Erik Satie

Titles in the series Critical Lives present the work of leading cultural figures of the modern period. Each book explores the life of the artist, writer, philosopher or architect in question and relates it to their major works.

In the same series

Michel Foucault
David Macey

Jean Genet
Stephen Barber

Pablo Picasso
Mary Ann Caws

Franz Kafka
Sander L. Gilman

Marcel Duchamp
Caroline Cros

Guy Debord
Andy Merrifield

Frank Lloyd Wright
Robert McCarter

Jean-Paul Sartre
Andrew Leak

James Joyce
Andrew Gibson

Noam Chomsky
Wolfgang B. Sperlich

Jorge Luis Borges
Jason Wilson

Ludwig Wittgenstein
Edward Kanterian

Erik Satie

Mary E. Davis

REAKTION BOOKS

Published by Reaktion Books Ltd
33 Great Sutton Street
London EC1V 0DX, UK

www.reaktionbooks.co.uk

First published 2007

Printed and bound in Great Britain
by Cromwell Press, Trowbridge, Wiltshire

British Library Cataloguing in Publication Data
Davis, Mary Elizabeth
    Erik Satie. – (Critical lives)
    1. Satie, Erik, 1866–1925
    I. Title
    780.9'2

    ISBN-13: 978 1 86189 321 5
    ISBN-10: 1 86189 321 3

Contents

Erik Satie photographed in 1922 by Man Ray.

Introduction

Satie (Alfred Erik Leslie-Satie, *dit* Erik). French composer, born in
Honfleur (1866 – 1925), author of *Trois Gymnopédies* for piano (1888),
the ballet *Parade* (1917) and *Socrate* (oratorio, 1918). His stripped-down
style is often humorous.
Le Petit Larousse Illustré

Erik Satie, cultivator of minimalist aesthetics, would have warmed
to this crisp biography in the *Petit Larousse Illustré*, the dictionary
that traces its roots to 1856 and stakes its claim as the premier
French guide to the 'evolution of the language and the world'. The
brief description conveys much about Satie for anyone who reads
between its three concise lines: a quirky personality comes across
in the spelling of his name – 'Erik' with a 'k' rather than the
conventional 'c'; the mention of Honfleur sets the scene in a
picturesque Norman port town and conjures a lineage of native
artists ranging from landscape painter Emile Boudin to novelist
Gustave Flaubert. The three referenced works trace a history of the
arts in Paris – from the cabarets of *fin-de-siècle* Montmartre, where
Satie presented himself as a 'gymnopédiste', to the Théâtre du
Châtelet, where Diaghilev's Ballets Russes gave a scandalous
performance of *Parade* at the height of World War I, to fashionable
salons of the Parisian elite where the classicizing 'symphonic

drama' *Socrate* was premiered in its aftermath. As for his 'stripped-down style' and humour, both emerge from the mingling of high art and vernacular culture that was central to Satie's sound – and to the history of modernist art. Thus considered, the *Petit Larousse Illustré* entry on Satie comes into focus as a tantalizing glimpse of man, music and legacy, all accomplished in under fifty words.

Longer accounts of Satie's life and work have been available since 1932, when Pierre-Daniel Templier published the first biography of the composer.[1] Templier had a close vantage point: his father, Alexandre, was Satie's friend and neighbour in the Paris suburb of Arcueil, and they were both involved in its Radical-Socialist Committee. The younger Templier's biography appeared in a series of studies devoted to 'Masters of Ancient and Modern Music', thus placing Satie in the company of Beethoven, Wagner, and Mozart as well as Debussy and Stravinsky. Illustrated with photographs and documents supplied by Satie's brother Conrad, the book's stated aim was 'authenticity': written not even a decade after Satie's death, it was an attempt to create a more realistic portrait of a composer who had been both hailed as 'the greatest musician in the world' and vilified as an untalented provocateur.[2] Templier offered a two-part assessment, covering details of Satie's life in the first section of his book and presenting a richly annotated chronology of works in the second. For the next sixteen years, during which the composer faded from public memory and largely disappeared from concert-hall and recital programmes, this volume was the primary available source on Satie, and even today it remains the authoritative study of his early years.

While Satie's star waned in France, the publication of Rollo Myers's English-language biography in 1948 fuelled interest in the composer in the United States and Britain.[3] By that time a number of significant composers and critics had already emerged as advocates for Satie, championing both his musical innovations and original voice. Virgil Thomson, a leader in the effort, famously acclaimed Satie as the originator of the 'only twentieth-century aesthetic in the Western World', and argued that the composer was 'the only one whose works can be enjoyed and appreciated without any knowledge of the history of music'.[4] John Cage, another unwavering admirer, pronounced Satie 'indispensable' and acclaimed him as 'art's most serious servant'.[5] Perhaps most importantly, in essays, concerts and his own compositions, Cage brought Satie to the attention of the postwar American avant-garde across the arts and promoted his aesthetic as a powerful alternative to more hermetic modes of modernism – an antidote to the control-orientated approaches of Schoenberg, Boulez and Stockhausen.

In a surprising manner, the cultural shifts of the 1950s and '60s further raised Satie's profile and saw the spread of his music in concert halls and less likely venues, including jazz clubs and rock festivals. His mass popularity arguably reached a high point when the rock group Blood, Sweat and Tears adapted two of the *Gymnopédies* and featured the recording as the lead track on their self-titled album in 1969; the album sold three million copies and won the Grammy Foundation's award for Album of the Year, while 'Variations on a Theme by Erik Satie' won the Grammy for Best Contemporary Instrumental Performance. The foundation for this crossover had been laid by historian Roger Shattuck's groundbreaking study *The Banquet Years* (1958, revised 1968), which solidified Satie's position as an avatar of modernism and an exemplar of hipness by situating the composer alongside Guillaume Apollinaire, Alfred Jarry and Henri Rousseau as one of the original members of the French avant-garde.[6] The group, Shattuck proposed, constituted the core of 'the fluid state known as bohemia, a cultural underground smacking of failure and fraud [that] crystallized for a few decades into a self-conscious avant-garde that carried the arts into a period of astonishingly varied renewal and accomplishment.'[7] For readers of the time, Satie's status as a progenitor of experimental art music – as well as rock music performed by bands styled in the image of their Parisian avant-garde forebears – was secured.

A seemingly reactionary response to this understanding of Satie as an icon of nonconformist chic set in as the century came to a close. A spate of specialized musicological studies, based on examinations of Satie's manuscripts and sketches, laid out the first comprehensive analysis of his work, from which emerged a fresh recognition of his contributions as well as a new awareness of his rigorous compositional technique. As the focus shifted from biography to compositional process, a consensus began to form about his importance not just for the avant-garde, but also for figures more fully assimilated into the musical mainstream, including Claude Debussy and Igor Stravinsky. No longer perceived as simply a musical eccentric, he was absorbed into the longer chain of music history, linked to Mozart and Rossini as well as Cage and Steve Reich. The view of Satie was further enlarged by the appearance of a steady stream of books exploring non-musical aspects of his creative work, and particularly his literary output; from the appearance of edited collections of his writings in 1981 to the arrival of his 'almost complete' correspondence in 2002, Satie's own views and idiosyncratic modes of expression could be factored with minimal mediation into the mix of evidence about his life and work.

Satie was a prolific and original writer, and although much of his work remained unpublished until recently, a number of his essays and commentaries saw print in specialized music journals as well as mass-market magazines in France and the United States during his lifetime. Among these were autobiographical sketches written at various times in his career, all of which are remarkable because they convey a considerable amount of information despite their almost complete lack of facts and overarching tone of irony. The first of these profiles, entitled 'Who I Am', initiated the series that Satie called 'Memories of an Amnesiac', which appeared between 1912 and 1914 in the *Revue musicale S.I.M.*.[8] 'Everyone will tell you that I am not a musician', Satie began; 'That is true':

From the outset of my career, I have classed myself among the phonometrographers. My works are pure phonometrics . . . Scientific thought dominates. As for the rest, I find greater pleasure in measuring a sound than in hearing it. With my phonometer in hand, I work happily and confidently. What can't I measure or weigh? All of Beethoven, all of Verdi, etc. It's very curious.[9]

A year later, in a brief description prepared for his publisher, Satie presented a different image, proclaiming himself a 'fantaisiste', thus aligning his work with that of a group of young poets led by Francis Carco and Tristan Klingsor. Identifying himself as 'the strangest musician of our time', he proceeded to state his importance: 'Short-sighted by birth, I am long-sighted by nature . . . We should not forget that the master is considered, by a great number of "young" composers, as the precursor and apostle of the musical revolution now taking place.'[10]

And even just before his death he struck a similar obfuscating tone, tinged with a sense of bitterness:

Life became so impossible for me that I resolved to retire to my estates and pass the remainder of my days in an ivory tower – or one of some other (metallic) metal. That is why I acquired a taste for misanthropy, why I cultivated hypochondria; why I became the most miserable (leaden) of men. It upset people to look at me – even through hallmarked gold eye-glasses. Yes. All this happened to me because of Music.[11]

Phonometrographer, *fantaisiste*, misanthrope: as these sketches attest, Satie was sharply aware of the power of image, and he worked throughout his career to hone and project a variety of carefully cultivated public personas. The ironic stance of his self-descriptions was matched by the unconventionality of his changing self-presentations – a process that began in his youth and endured to his death. These shifts are documented in photographs and self-portraits, as well as in drawings and paintings of Satie done by friends in the course of his life: from Augustin Grass-Mick's *fin-de-siècle* depiction of the composer in the company of stars including Jane Avril and Toulouse-Lautrec, to the portraits done in the 1920s by Pablo Picasso, Jean Cocteau and Francis Picabia. As these artworks attest, Satie perceived the link between public image and professional recognition, and throughout his career manipulated his look to conform to his artistic aims. A few examples make the case: working in the cabarets of Montmartre as a young man, he adopted a Bohemian uniform, then took to wearing one of seven identical velvet suits at all times; as the composer of pseudo-spiritual music in the 1890s he founded his own church and roamed the streets dressed in priestly cassocks; as a well-known figure in the avant-garde he wore a dark three-piece suit more typical of a bourgeois functionary than a revolutionary. In short, it is clear that Satie self-consciously projected variable identities through his appearance as well as his art, creating a mutually reinforcing relationship between personality and vocation.

This biography, one tale among many that could be told about the composer, takes Satie's purposeful meshing of public image and artistic enterprise as the backdrop for consideration of his career. Against the screen of his dramatic shifts in wardrobe and changing self-presentations, his work and legacy come into fresh perspective. In an age when the celebrity culture we now take for granted was but an emerging phenomenon, Satie clearly understood the value of cutting a unique – and easily recognizable – figure. Clothes helped make the man, and they surely played a role in articulating the main breakthroughs in his art.

1

Honfleur

I came very young into a world that was very old.
Satie

Musing on his family origins in 1924, Satie speculated that, while
the roots of the family tree might 'reach back into the mists of
time', the branches probably did not include members with
'connections to the Nobility (even Papal)' but instead were filled
with 'good modest serfs, which in the past was an honour and a
pleasure (for the serf's good lord, I mean).'[1] His own story begins
modestly enough on Honfleur's rue Haute, which contrary to its
name is the lowest street in the town. The Saties were longstanding residents of Honfleur, having lived on that same street
probably since 1817, when Erik's great-grandfather, François-
Jacques-Amable Satie, first arrived.[2] A broken piece of ceramic
bearing the name Guillaume Satie provides evidence that the group
was in Normandy by 1725, and once there they did not leave:
Pierre-François (1734–1811) settled in the port town of Le Havre,
where his eldest son Joseph-André (b. 1771) remained, while the
younger François-Jacques-Amable (b. 1780) crossed the harbour
and relocated in Honfleur. Both sons distinguished themselves as
sea-captains, as did François-Jacques-Amable's son Jules-André
(1816–1886). Jules, as he was known, married the reportedly stern
Strasbourg-born Eulalie Fornton, who bore the couple three
children: Marie-Marguerite (b. 1875, listed in the Honfleur records

The garden and house of the Satie family in Honfleur.

as having 'disappeared to America'), Louis-Adrien (1843–1907), and Jules-Alfred (1842–1903).[3]

The brothers, known as Adrien and Alfred, remained in Honfleur and continued to work in the family shipping business before pursuing other careers. Templier reports that they had 'opposite characters': while Adrien, nicknamed 'Sea Bird', was 'undisciplined', Alfred was 'studious and docile'.[4] As a young man Alfred matriculated at the college in Lisieux, where he met Albert Sorel, the historian and author who later served as Secretary to the President of the French Senate; the two remained friends late into life. It was to Sorel that Alfred wrote in March 1865 with news of his whirlwind decision to marry. 'My Dear Albert,' he began:

The news I am about to give you will cause you no jubilation. I am on the point of marrying . . . guess who! You will never guess – Miss Jeannie Leslie Anton!!! . . . We have met only three times at Miss Walworth's; we write to each other every day, and what letters! Everything was done by correspondence and in two weeks![5]

Jane Anton, known as 'Jeannie' to her family, was a London-born girl who had come to Honfleur to study French and acquire the continental polish considered desirable for young ladies. A potential barrier to her marriage to Alfred was her Anglican faith; as the would-be bridegroom noted in his letter to Sorel, 'among their difficulties' the 'religious one' was hardly the least, since his mother – a staunch Catholic – was insisting on Jane's promise to raise any children in that faith. Jane refused, and in the end the couple wed on 19 July at the Anglican church of St Mary, Barnes, outside London. 'The respectable Saties', Templier reports, 'Catholics and anglophobes', and the 'worthy Antons' examined one another 'in silence, frostily'.[6] A honeymoon followed in Scotland, the childhood home of Jane's mother Elsie, and upon their return to Honfleur Jane and Alfred announced the impending birth of their first child. At 9 a.m. on 17 May 1866 Eric-Alfred Leslie was born; three months later he was taken to the Anglican church and baptized. The earliest known photograph shows him as a baby, perhaps two years old, with a shock of hair (which was red) and a round, smiling face, wearing an embroidered dress typical of the region and looking directly into the camera.

Three other children completed the family: Louise-Olga-Jeannie (1868–1948), Conrad (1869–1933) and Diane (1871–1872). With each Anglican baptism the animosity between Jane and her mother-in-law escalated, and by all accounts the situation became untenable while Alfred was away from home, serving as a lieutenant in the National Guard during the Franco-Prussian War. When he returned to Honfleur it was only to pack up; by the end of 1871 the family had

Erik Satie at about two years old, *c.* 1868.

settled in Paris, where Sorel had arranged a position for Alfred, who spoke seven languages, as a government translator.[7]

Tragic events followed on the heels of this move. Diane, four months old, died shortly after the relocation, and in October 1872 Jane died suddenly aged 34. Alfred, disconsolate, departed for a year of European travel, leaving his children in the care of relatives; Olga was sent to live with a maternal uncle in Le Havre, while Eric and Conrad were taken in by their paternal grandparents, accepted only on Eulalie's condition that they renounce the Anglican faith and be re-baptized in the Catholic Church. Eric – now aged six and judged old enough to be more or less on his own – was placed as a boarder at the Collège of Honfleur, located just two streets away from the rue Haute, where he passed the next six years. The school guaranteed students instruction in 'all things moral and healthy', a category that encompassed religion, reading, writing, French, English, German, history, geography, arithmetic, literature, algebra, trigonometry, physics and chemistry, along with hygiene, gymnastics, art and music.[8] The rigorous curriculum was the centrepiece of a regimented life; accommodations were spare and students wore uniforms that consisted of short trousers, white shirts and a dark jacket. Satie later recounted these years without nostalgia. 'I stayed in that city until I was twelve years old,' he recalled, 'I had an unremarkable childhood and adolescence, with no features worth recording in serious writings.'[9]

A mediocre student at best, Satie did well in Latin and showed a talent for music, to the extent that he was given the somewhat odd yet musical nickname 'Crin-Crin', which translates roughly as 'scraper'. Within months of his return to Honfleur his grandparents arranged lessons for him with the town's most notable musician, Gustave Vinot, the organist at the church of St Léonard. Vinot had distinguished himself as a student of Gregorian chant and early music at the Ecole Niedermeyer, the conservative school that specialized in training church musicians, and during four years of lessons with him Satie no doubt studied chant and solfège as well as piano and organ. The instructions perhaps went further afield; Vinot was also a composer of light music, including a piece entitled *La Valse des Patineurs*, which he performed to general acclaim with the Honfleur Philharmonic in the 1870s, and he may have introduced his pupil to some of the techniques and methods of popular music. In any event, for the young Satie the surroundings must have been as enchanting as the subject matter, as St Léonard was one of the oldest and most elaborate buildings in town, with a tower and nave dating to the fifteenth century, and a decorated west portal that was recognized as one of the last expressions of Gothic art. Largely destroyed in the Hundred Years' War, it had been rebuilt in the seventeenth century, in the process gaining a distinctive octagonal bell tower decorated with detailed bas-reliefs depicting musical instruments.

Vinot left Honfleur for a post in Lyon in 1878, but the year marked more than the end of Satie's music lessons: that summer his grandmother drowned while taking her regular swim at the town beach, and Eric and his brother Conrad were returned to their father's care. Alfred had settled in Paris, and when his sons joined him there he took an unconventional approach to their education, declining to enrol them in school but instead taking them to lectures at the Collège de France and the Sorbonne, to performances of operettas and plays at his favorite theatres, and to Versailles for Sunday dinners hosted by Sorel. This period, which must have been an idyllic reprieve for Eric after the discipline of his life in Honfleur, lasted less than a year. At Sorel's house Alfred met Eugénie Barnetche, a composer and a serious pianist who had studied at the Paris Conservatoire, and after a brief courtship they married in January 1879. Ten years her husband's senior, Eugénie's influence in the household was considerable: among other things she compelled the family, now extended to include her mother, to move to a new home on the rue de Constantinople, near the Gare St Lazare.[10] As she took charge of Eric and Conrad's education, one of her first priorities was to ensure that Eric continued music lessons. Enrolling him in the preparatory class of Emile Descombes at the Conservatoire, she initiated what would be a seven-year course of study and a source of continual frustration for her stepson.

The Paris Conservatoire offered a music curriculum that differed dramatically from the programme Satie had followed with Vinot, as well as an atmosphere far less inspiring than the eclectic décor at St Léonard. Satie later described it as a 'huge, very uncomfortable, and rather ugly building, a sort of local penitentiary, without exterior charm – or interior, either'.[11] The nation's premier school for the training of musicians had by the late nineteenth century become a stodgy institution known primarily for its rigour and insistence on technical excellence. Admission was highly competitive, thus by the age of thirteen Satie's piano skills must have been more than adequate; his audition piece was a Chopin Ballade, and during his first year he performed virtuosic concertos by Ferdinand Hiller and Felix Mendelssohn to the satisfaction of the faculty. The problem was not technique or musicality but attitude, encapsulated in the assessment of one faculty member who deemed him 'gifted but indolent'. In 1881 a performance of a Mendelssohn concerto prompted his own teacher to evaluate Satie as the 'laziest student in the Conservatoire', and a lacklustre performance of Beethoven's Sonata in A flat major (Op. 26) in 1882, probably at the end-of-semester jury, was the final straw: Satie was dismissed from the school and sent home.[12]

In the midst of his son's dramas, Alfred Satie made a career change. In 1881 he opened a stationery store, where he sold sheet music as well as writing paper and no doubt with his wife's encouragement, he acquired the catalogue of the music publisher Wiart, which had printed a number of Eugénie's compositions. The following year he began to publish music himself, including her *Scherzo* (Op. 86), *Rêverie* (Op. 66) and *Boléro* (Op. 88). Alfred also tried his own hand at composition, producing a polka entitled *Souvenir d'Honfleur* in 1883 and, in total, a group of thirteen works by 1890. Perhaps in the hope of furthering this enterprise, he moved his family and business several times in the early 1880s, settling finally on the Boulevard de Magenta, in the hub of the Parisian music industry.[13] He also began to cultivate contacts in Parisian music halls and café-concerts and found some success publishing chansons and other light fare heard in these venues. Alfred's association seems to have been closest with the Eldorado, the Scala and the Eden-Concert, but he also published songs popularized in larger establishments such as the Ambassadeurs, the Alcazar d'Hiver and the Bataclan, by stars including Marius Ricard and the famous Mademoiselle Blockette.[14] It seems likely that Satie would have accompanied his father as he visited these spots in search of new tunes, but it is impossible to know for sure.

In any event, surrounded by musical activity at home and prompted by his stepmother, Satie returned to the Conservatoire in 1883, this time as an *auditeur* in Antoine Taudou's class on harmony. The experience seems to have been more stimulating than piano study, since within a year Satie produced his first composition, a brief piano piece with the nondescript title *Allegro*. This seemingly inconsequential work – it consists of only nine bars of music – offers a surprising glimpse of Satie's future compositional style. Dated 'Honfleur, September 1884' and composed during a holiday visit to his hometown, the piece includes a fragment of the widely known tune 'Ma Normandie', which was written by Frédéric Bérat in 1836. So popular that it became the 'unofficial anthem of Normandy', the song is a paean to the charms of the north country. Satie quotes a bit of the refrain, the lyrics of which are 'I long to see my Normandy once again, It's the country where I saw the light of day', in the centre of his composition. The musical reference, clear enough to be audible to any listener familiar with the tune, creates an allusion to both song and place, thus deepening the experience of the music beyond the purely sonic realm into the arena of memory and nostalgia. The musical borrowing also suggests Alfred's role, since such techniques were a staple of performances in the music halls and café-concerts he routinely frequented.

The little *Allegro*, which Satie signed, for the first time, with the name 'Erik', remained unpublished until the 1970s and was unknown in Satie's lifetime. Instead, Satie made his public debut as a composer in 1887 with two simple piano pieces composed in 1885, which were published in a supplement to the magazine *La Musique des familles*. His *Valse-Ballet* (later issued by his father as Satie's Op. 62) appeared in March and his *Fantaisie-Valse* in July. Bearing a dedication to 'Contamine de Latour', this last piece heralds the arrival of an important and eccentric personality and influence in Satie's life and signals the start of a new phase in his fledgling career.

2

Student, Soldier, Gymnopédiste

I lost no time in developing an unpleasant (original) originality,
irrelevant, anti-French, unnatural . . .
Satie

José Maria Vincente Ferrer, Francisco de Paula, Patricio Manuel
Contamine – known as Patrice Contamine to most of his friends,
and as J.P. Contamine de Latour or 'Lord Cheminot' in his
professional life – had come to Paris in the 1880s from the
Catalonian town of Tarragona, located just south of Barcelona.
Born on 17 March 1867, he was exactly ten months younger than
Satie and, like the composer, in his early twenties had become
captivated by the *vie de bohème* lived by artists and entertainers in
the city's countercultural mecca: Montmartre. They met in 1885,
probably on the Butte, and as Latour later recalled, were from the
outset 'joined in fraternal friendship':

> We were inseparable, spending our days and part of our nights
> together, exchanging ideas, planning ambitious projects,
> dreaming of sensational successes, growing drunk on crazy
> hopes and laughing at our own poverty. I could say we lived out
> the final scenes of Murger's *La Bohème*, transplanted from the
> Latin Quarter to Montmartre. We didn't eat every day, but we
> never missed an aperitif; I remember a particular pair of
> trousers and a pair of shoes that used to pass from one to the

other, and which we had to mend every morning . . . It was a happy life.[1]

Latour aimed to make a career as a poet and short-story writer, and his imagination was fertile: he claimed, among other things, to be a descendant of Napoleon and a rightful heir to the French crown. Satie began to set poems by the friend he jokingly nicknamed 'Le Vieux Modeste' almost immediately, starting with the melancholy 'Elégie', a brief lament on lost hope, in 1886. Settings of sentimental poems – 'Les Anges', 'Les Fleurs' and 'Sylvie' – followed that year; rife with hothouse images of 'angels floating in the ether like lilies' and 'lutes shimmering in divine harmony', they reflect Latour's lingering attraction to Baudelaire and the Symbolists. Satie, eschewing more predictable approaches such as chromaticism and Wagnerian excess, matched these verses with music that in an understated and original way mirrored their decadent quality. His simple and fluid melodies recalled the modal sounds of the ancient past, his delicate harmonies were built from colouristic seventh, ninth and eleventh chords presented in static, slow repetition. Further, he took the radical step of eliminating both the time signature and bar lines from his score in 'Sylvie', thus announcing his break with convention in no uncertain terms and initiating a practice that would become a hallmark of his style. His father, no doubt intending to confer a degree of legitimacy on these offbeat works, published 'Elégie' as Satie's 'Op. 19' in 1887 and collected the three other settings as *Trois Mélodies* of 'Op. 20' that same year, suggesting a compositional history that simply did not exist.

Roaming Paris with Latour in the late 1880s, Satie became increasingly fascinated with Gothic art and architecture. There was much to absorb: from the 1840s onward the architect and theorist Eugène-Emmanuel Viollet-le-Duc (1814–1879) had worked to restore the many monuments that had been damaged in the Revolution, including the cathedral of Notre Dame, the Hôtel de

Satie in his late teens, *c.* 1884.

Cluny and the Abbey of Saint-Denis. These restorations, while controversial, were a revelation for the young composer, inspiring a change of affect and signalling a new direction in his work. Neglecting the Conservatoire, where he remained enrolled in the intermediate piano class of George Mathias, he spent his days meditating in the gloom of Notre Dame and reading medieval history at the Bibliothèque Nationale, passing hours 'passionately thumbing through Viollet-le-Duc's weighty tomes'.[2] A new piety seized him, he 'affected a great humility' and 'talked endlessly about "his religion", the strict commandments of which were meticulously followed'.[3] Nicknamed 'Monsieur le Pauvre' by friends who observed this turn toward earnest austerity, he cultivated a new aesthetic in his compositions, aiming to translate medieval style to the musical realm. The first works in this vein, entitled *Ogives,* made the intended connection clear through their invocation of the technical term for the pointed arches typical of Gothic architecture; according his younger brother Conrad, they were inspired in the course of 'hours of ecstasy' at Notre Dame

A stereoscopic photo, *c.* 1900, of a chimera on the north tower of Notre-Dame cathedral; in the distance is Montmartre.

during which Satie's 'thoughts used to follow the curves of the vaulting and rise toward the Creator'.[4]

Four brief compositions for piano, the *Ogives* build on the innovations of the Latour songs, but their explicitly historicizing subject provided Satie with a new grounding for his musical experiments. Fluid modal melodies notated without bar lines now suggest plainchant, while slow parallel harmonic motion calls to mind the early polyphony known as organum. In addition, the four-phrase structure of each *Ogive* evokes medieval performance practice traditions: in the first phrase the basic tune is presented in open octaves, suggesting the intonation of the chant melody by a soloist, while the following phrases offer variant voicings and slightly different harmonizations, mimicking the response of a choir, congregation and/or instrumentalist. This antiphonal effect is intensified by Satie's alternation of textures and his treatment of dynamics, with dramatic shifts from pianissimo to fortissimo at each change of phrase. In short, by mining the past to make the *Ogives* thematically meaningful, Satie expanded on his new repertoire of musical approaches, going beyond issues of style to the broader parameters of form.

As Satie became more deeply engrossed in composition, his enthusiasm for the Conservatoire plummeted to a new low; as Conrad Satie explained, 'a Christian idealist like Satie could not find fulfilment' in such an institution, and 'his lofty soul underwent peculiar suffering at finding itself enclosed in sterile academic formulae'.[5] The situation was little more acceptable to the Conservatoire faculty, who judged his performances in 1886 to be 'very insignificant' and 'laborious', and in June that year his teacher Mathias bluntly deemed his presentation of a Mendelssohn Prelude 'worthless'.[6] By the end of November Satie had volunteered for his mandatory military duty and left the Conservatoire for good; in December he departed Paris for Arras with the 33rd Infantry Regiment. Enlisted for a three-year stint, he barely made it through four months of service. As Templier reports, 'he was soon tired of this new life', and took 'drastic steps' to escape: 'One winter evening he lay out under the stars with no shirt on. Serious bronchitis ensued, followed by convalescence and further convalescence; he was left in peace for nearly three months.'[7]

Satie's illness guaranteed his release from the military, which came in November 1887. The months leading up to this formal discharge were spent in Paris, where he read Gustave Flaubert's novels, including *Salammbô* and *La Tentation de Saint Antoine*, and attended the opera, where he saw Chabrier's *Le Roi malgré lui*. Latour remained a major presence; Satie set another of his poems, 'Chanson', and seems to have been inspired to write his first suite of dances, *Trois Sarabandes*, after reading Latour's poem *La Perdition*; in his manuscript copy of the work, an excerpt of the verse written most likely in Latour's hand appears in the upper left-hand corner of the first piece. The vaguely Symbolist poem sets an apocalyptic tone:

Suddenly all was revealed and the damned fell
Shrieking and jostling in a whirl as they were thrown;

And when in starless night they found themselves alone
They thought each other black, so began to blaspheme.

The three miniature pieces in Satie's set seem to owe more of a debt to the venerable dance that inspired their title than to Latour's dark images. The sarabande, which originated in sixteenth-century Spain, was assimilated as an inherently French instrumental genre during the seventeenth century, danced in intimate and simple settings as well as in the courtly splendour of Louis XIV's Versailles. Crossing the history of the genre with his own ongoing explorations of modality and rhythmic stasis, Satie created works that have since been acclaimed as milestones, the harbingers of a 'new aesthetic, instituting a particular atmosphere, a totally original magic of sound'.[8] Indeed, the *Sarabandes* introduce compositional approaches that would prove important not only in Satie's later work but also in the broader history of French music. First, they presented a new conception of large-scale form, in which groups of three very similar pieces, deliberately interlinked by means of motivic cells, harmonic events and recurring interval patterns, combine to constitute a unified work. This was an alternative to traditions largely associated with nineteenth-century German music – including sonata form, theme and variations, and the like – and in Satie's view amounted to an 'absolutely new form' that was 'good in itself'.[9] Second, the *Sarabandes* proposed a new compositional system in which motivic cells were repeated or juxtaposed; this, too, was a rejection of Germanic preferences for melodic development and variation. Finally, the work subverted the convention of associating dissonance and consonance with longing and resolution – cornerstones of the tonal system, exploited to an extreme by Richard Wagner and late-Romantic German composers – by suppressing altogether notions of such emotional strain. The essential 'Frenchness' in Satie's work was especially evident in his first drafts of the compositions, which followed the model of *ancien régime* sarabandes in their bipartite design, with the first section concluding on a dangling dominant chord and the division articulated by a repeat sign.[10] A more contemporary French reference for Satie may have been the Chabrier opera he saw just before he began work on the composition; much has been made by scholars of the way in which the *Sarabandes* include chains of consecutive ninth chords similar to those in the prelude to *Le Roi malgré lui*.[11] Satie was clearly an admirer of Chabrier, and after hearing that opera was so 'carried away with enthusiasm for the composer's daring' that he was moved to leave an ornate copy of one of his own works, 'decorated with a superb dedication – in red ink, of course', with Chabrier's concièrge as a token of his esteem.[12] Alas, Chabrier seems never to have responded to this extravagant gesture.

Shortly after his official military discharge was issued Satie left his family home on the Boulevard de Magenta and took up residence in Montmartre. The departure may have been precipitated by an argument with his father and stepmother that followed the younger Satie's affair with the family maid; in any case, a gift of 1600 francs from his father financed the rental and furnishing of an apartment at 50 rue Condorcet.[13] Freed from responsibilities to either Conservatoire or Army, Satie embraced the bohemian lifestyle that flourished on the Butte at the *fin de siècle*, frequenting its many cabarets and cafés, and associating with the poets, painters and musicians who likewise gravitated to its alternative entertainments. Headquarters for many of these artists was the Chat Noir, an 'artistic cabaret' founded in 1881 by Rodolphe Salis, a student at the Ecole des Beaux-Arts who billed his establishment as 'the most extraordinary cabaret in the world', where one could 'rub shoulders with the most famous men of Paris . . . with foreigners from every corner of the world.'[14] A small, two-room space that could barely accommodate 30 people, the original

LE CHAT NOIR
Caveau Artistique
68, Boulevard de Clichy
PARIS-MONTMARTRE

The Chat Noir after its move to the Boulevard de Clichy in Montmartre.

Chat Noir was located on the Boulevard de Rochechouart, only a few minutes' walk from Satie's apartment; the exterior of the building was fitted out with a sign depicting a black cat, as well as a notice to passers-by instructing them to 'Stop . . . Be Modern!' Inside there was 'a mixture of fun and seriousness without doctrine', as patrons mingled in a decor loaded with faux-medieval and pseudo-Renaissance art and furniture, including rustic chairs, stained-glass windows, suits of armour and masks, imitation tapestries and an overwhelming amount of cat imagery. The front room was open to the general public, but the back room, known (in joking reference to the Académie de France) as the 'Institut', was an early VIP room, reserved for regulars; it also served as a workroom for production of the cabaret's own illustrated journal, *Le Chat noir*. Under editors Emile Goudeau and Alphonse Allais and artistic directors Henri Rivière and George Auriol, the journal

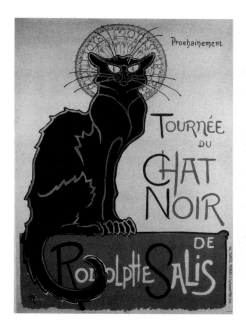

Tournée du Chat Noir: a poster of 1896 by Théophile Alexandre Steinlen for the Montmartre cabaret venue.

published social and political satire alongside illustrations by Adolphe Wilette, Caran d'Ache and Théophile-Alexandre Steinlen, among others. Still popular today is Steinlen's rendition of a rather sinister black cat perched on a red stone slab, which served as a publicity poster for the cabaret.

The journal was not the only outlet for Chat Noir expressiveness. Salis, defying a government statute that prohibited music in cabarets – thus distinguishing them from cafés and the café-concert, where musical performances were expected – installed a piano at the Chat Noir and began to feature song as well as poetry and verse at his evening shows. After he acquired a larger space a few blocks away on the rue Laval, the slate of entertainments expanded to include shadow plays, which were presented in a theatre on the building's top floor. On the evening of 28 December 1887 a shadow play of unprecedented ambition and

Henri Rivière, photo of technicians moving shadow puppets behind the screen at the Chat Noir, Montmartre.

opulence had its premiere; this was Rivière's adaptation of Flaubert's *Tentation de Saint Antoine*, rendered in 40 scenes and billed as a 'féerie à grand spectacle'. The first shadow play to use colour projections, it featured musical accompaniment by an ensemble that included an organ (or harmonium) and four percussionists, and involved two narrators, each of whom played the role of a 'choeur antique'.[15] This premiere seems to have occasioned Satie's initial visit to the Chat Noir as well as his introduction to Salis. As Latour recalled the moment, Satie's friend Vital Hocquet, a plumber who published poetry under the pseudonym Narcisse Lebeau, 'announced imposingly "Erik Satie, gymnopédiste!" to which Salis, bowing as low as he could, replied: "That's a very fine profession!"'[16]

Satie, who at the time of this meeting had at best made preliminary sketches for the works that would become the famous *Gymnopédies*, had in a stroke found an identity and a new second home. Certainly he would have warmed to the Chat's eclectic décor, so precisely in tune with his own fascinations with the past, and he must have been delighted to fit into a clique of regulars that included a number of fellow Normans, notably Allais, who although a decade older than Satie had lived on the same street in Honfleur and attended the same boarding school. In addition there were the painters Georges de Feure and Marcellin Desboutin, poets Charles Cros and Jean Richepin, singers Paul Delmet, Maurice Mac-Nab and Vincent Hyspa, and the notorious Aristide Bruant, whose gruff stage manner matched the off-colour lyrics he performed. Within weeks of his first visit Satie was hired as the cabaret's 'second pianist', replacing Dynam-Victor Fumet. This new post, and more generally the Chat Noir milieu, inspired a major change of affect in Satie; Latour recalled that the composer, 'till then shy and reserved, gave free reign to the hoard of wild good humour that lay dormant in him'.[17] He changed his appearance entirely and, following a 'chatnoiresque rite', let his beard and hair grow long. As for wardrobe, Latour recalled that Satie destroyed the few garments he owned in a frenzy:

> One day he took his clothes, rolled them into a ball, sat on them, dragged them across the floor, trod on them and drenched them with all kinds of liquid until he'd turned them into complete rags; he dented his hat, broke up his shoes, tore his tie to ribbons and replaced his fine linen with fearful flannel shirts.[18]

In the wake of this purge, Satie began to sport the uniform of Bohemian Paris, wearing a top hat and a large Windsor tie along with dark trousers and a long frock coat. As his friend Francis Jourdain, the decorative artist and furniture-maker, recalled, the composer became a 'dandy, of the sort who, as you might imagine, notices the dictates of fashion only so that he can violate them'.[19] Signalling a new association with the radical fringe, this sartorial

Santiago Rusiñol's sketch of Satie at the harmonium, 1891.

shift was the first of many reinventions Satie would make via fashion, and as Latour noted, it was emblematic of Satie's decision to 'forge a personal artistic style for himself'.[20]

The Chat Noir proved a stimulus to Satie's work as well as the inspiration for a new look; by 2 April 1888 the composer had completed his most ambitious composition to date, the *Trois Gymnopédies* for piano. The source of this unusual title, a translation of the Greek word describing a yearly festival at which young men danced naked (or perhaps simply unarmed), remains the subject of speculation. His friend Roland-Manuel maintained that Satie adopted it after reading *Salammbô*, while Templier and others have attributed the inspiration to Latour, noting that an extract from his poem *Les Antiques* was published with the score of the first piece in the magazine *La Musique des familles* in the summer of 1888. Latour's poetry, with its reference to 'atoms of amber, glistening in the firelight' that 'joined their sarabande to the gymnopédie' surely makes the connection explicit, but there is no certainty that the musical score did not precede the poem.[21] Satie may simply have landed on the idea while perusing the *Larousse Illustré* or a more specialized music reference book such as Dominique Mondo's *Dictionnaire de Musique*, which defined 'gymnopédie' as a 'nude dance, accompanied by song, which youthful Spartan maidens danced on specific occasions', following the similar definition in Jean-Jacques Rousseau's 1768 *Dictionnaire de la Musique*. Whatever the origins of the title, there can be no doubt that the compositions reflect Satie's integration of Chat Noir aesthetics into the idiosyncratic style he had under development.

Like the *Sarabandes*, the *Gymnopédies* evoke a dance tradition, this time calling up ideas of the waltz via their steady triple metre. Although the melodies still have a modal flavour – perhaps Satie's attempt to suggest the music of ancient Greece – they are matched to a patterned chordal accompaniment much in the manner of popular salon music. Ideas are repeated and juxtaposed, and harmonies are more restrained but still far from tonal; while there are many unresolved seventh chords, the composition does not include the more dissonant ninth and eleventh sonorities present in Satie's earlier compositions. The real innovation of the *Gymnopédies*, however, occurs in the area of form: Satie carries forward from the *Sarabandes* the idea of a three-part structure, in which the individual 'movements' are linked by shared material, but he treats the design with more nuance. This amounts to a wholesale shift of compositional approach; as Roger Shattuck notes, Satie 'takes one musical idea and . . . regards it briefly from three different directions. He varies . . . the notes in the melody but not its general shape, the chords in the accompaniment but not the dominant shape.'[22]

This emphasis on perspective rather than progress, on nuanced variation rather than development, is signalled in the performance indications for each of the *Gymnopédies*: 'Lent et douloureux', 'Lent et triste' and 'Lent et grave'. The result is an ethereal and atmospheric music that must have sounded right at home in the oddly appointed rooms of the Chat Noir. Announced in the cabaret's journal in November 1888, the third *Gymnopédie* was endorsed with irony-tinged enthusiasm: 'We cannot recommend this essentially artistic work highly enough to the musical public', the advertisement proclaimed, 'It may rightly be considered one of the most beautiful of the century that has witnessed the birth of this unfortunate gentleman.'[23]

The three *Gymnopédies* were published separately, over a period of years. In 1888, shortly after the first piece in the set appeared in *La Musique des familles*, the third was published privately by Dupré in a deluxe edition on fine paper, with the title in elaborate red Gothic letters.[24] The second did not see print until 1895, also in an

Satie's manuscript score for the first *Gymnopédie* (published in 1888).

edition by Dupré, and the set as a whole was published only in 1898. By that time Satie had befriended Claude Debussy, and the older composer had orchestrated Nos 1 and 3 of the set; the arrangements were completed in late 1896 and premiered on 20 February 1897 at a concert in the Salle Erard, with Gustave Doret conducting. This was a milestone in Satie's career, as the concert was sponsored by the prestigious Société Nationale de Musique – a state-sanctioned organization helmed by musical heavyweights including César Franck, Camille Saint-Saëns and Vincent d'Indy – which had not previously performed his work. It was also the only time in his career that Debussy orchestrated another composer's work, which attests to his high estimation for Satie at the time. Debussy apparently became intrigued with the idea of orchestrating his friend's compositions one evening when Satie was playing through the pieces for Doret. 'Pince-nez poised for the assault,' Doret recalled, Satie

> seated himself at the piano. But his playing was a good deal less than perfect and didn't do the pieces justice. 'Come on,' said Debussy, 'I'll show you what your music sounds like.' And under his miraculous fingers the heart of the *Gymnopédies*, with all their colours and nuances, was laid bare in an astonishing manner. 'The next thing', I said, 'is to orchestrate them *like that*.' 'I absolutely agree,' Debussy replied. 'If Satie doesn't object, I'll get down to it tomorrow.'[25]

Satie, of course, had no objection, and Debussy's orchestral version has remained a repertoire standard even while a range of other adaptations of the *Gymnopédies* have appeared and disappeared from the musical landscape with regularity. Satie gained considerable exposure with a mainstream audience thanks to the performance, but it must also have been frustrating, since Debussy received much of the credit for the work – to the extent that some critics claimed that he had completely transformed the pieces, an assertion belied by Satie's original score.

Such frictions were typical of Satie's friendship with Debussy, and yet this was one of the most enduring and complex associations of his life. The relationship between the two men has inspired considerable speculation over the years, not infrequently focused on Satie's sexual orientation and the possibility that their interaction included a romantic or physical dimension. Their contemporaries were circumspect about the issue; Louis Laloy, for example, who knew them both, maintained that they had a 'turbulent but indissoluble' friendship based in 'musical brotherhood'. More recently, Marc Bredel credibly argued in his 1982 psychological profile of Satie that the composer was a 'repressed homosexual' deeply attracted to Debussy.[26] Since no surviving letters or documents fully illuminate the nature of their personal relationship, the issue remains open to speculation, but there can be no doubt about their close working relationship and regular exchange of ideas. Slightly older than Satie but far more renowned in the early years of their friendship, Debussy not only provided his colleague with entrée into sanctioned musical circles such as the Société Nationale, but also introduced him to publishers and others in the Parisian music industry. For his part, and contrary to expectation, Satie seems to have prodded Debussy to explore new ideas and compositional approaches: his *Sarabandes* of 1887 were a model for Debussy's *Sarabande*, composed seven years later, and Debussy's children's ballet *La Boîte à Joujoux* of 1913 includes fragments of popular tunes and familiar opera extracts much in the manner of Satie's 1890s cabaret style. Perhaps best known, however, is the case of Debussy's opera *Pelléas et Mélisande*, premiered in 1902 but begun nearly a decade earlier. As reported by Cocteau in 1920, the work had its genesis thanks to Satie, who when asked by Debussy about his ongoing work, replied that he was considering a setting of the Belgian Symbolist Maurice

Maeterlinck's play *Princesse Maleine*, but did not know how to get the required authorization. 'Some days afterward,' Cocteau recounted, 'Debussy, having obtained the authorization of Maeterlinck, commenced *Pelléas et Mélisande*.'[27] In fact, Cocteau has confused the history: Debussy did write to Maeterlinck, but his request, for *Princess Maleine* (not *Pelléas*) was denied, as the work had already been promised to Vincent d'Indy. *Pelléas* came later, following Debussy's discovery of the play in 1893. In the broader sense, however, Satie did not hesitate to take some credit for Debussy's 'Impressionistic' aesthetic and remembered advising his friend to take a cue from visual art: 'Why not make use of the representational methods of Claude Monet, Cézanne, Toulouse-Lautrec and so on? Why not make musical transpositions of them? Nothing simpler . . . This was the starting point for experiments abounding in tentative – even fruitful – results.'[28]

While the matter of influence is debatable, and the details of the first encounter between the two composers remain lost to history, it is clear that the friendship was established by 1892. That year Debussy inscribed a copy of his *Cinq Poèmes de Baudelaire* to 'Erik Satie, gentle medieval musician strayed into this century for the joy of his friend C. A. Debussy', and Satie reciprocated by presenting Debussy with a copy of one of his recent compositions inscribed 'to the good old son Cl. A. Debussy from his brother in the Lord, Erik Satie'. A profile of Debussy that Satie wrote for *Vanity Fair* in 1922 would seem to fix the date of their introduction in 1891 or 1892: 'As soon as I saw him for the first time, I felt drawn towards him and longed to live forever at his side. For thirty years I had the joy of seeing this wish fulfilled . . . it seemed as if we had *always* known each other.'[29]

Satie's recollections would suggest that the two did not meet at the Conservatoire, even though both were students there from 1879 to 1884, but rather that they first crossed paths somewhere on Montmartre, where both were habitués of cabarets including the Chat Noir, the Divan japonais and the Auberge du Clou. Both were also regulars at the Librairie d'Art Indépendant, the bookshop specializing in esoteric and occult literature that was run by Edmond Bailly and frequented by Symbolist poets and avant-garde artists as well as modernist composers. As one of the shop's adherents, Victor-Emile Michelet, recalled, in the late 1880s Debussy 'arrived almost every day in the late afternoon, either alone or with the faithful Erik Satie'.[30] Yet another possible meeting place for the two composers was the Exposition Universelle in Paris in 1889, since, like most Parisians, Satie and Debussy paid repeated visits to this massive fair and each was affected by the music he heard there. Ensembles performing music and dance had been brought from far and wide to the French capital for this celebration of the centenary of the Revolution; the main attraction was the newly built Eiffel Tower, but crowds flocked to pavilions that featured performing groups from the United States, the Far East and the French colonies, as well as from other European cities and towns. A Javanese village reconstructed on the exhibition grounds, complete with a full gamelan and dance troupe, captured Debussy's imagination, while Satie gravitated to the performances given by visiting Romanian musicians. In July he sketched a four-bar 'Chanson hongroise' that aimed to capture the essence of their sound, and by early the following year this idea had blossomed into another set of three dances, which he gave the umbrella label *Gnossiennes*.

At about this same time Satie appears to have made his first contributions to journals published by the cabarets he patronized. An unsigned advertisement for the *Ogives* that ran in the February 1889 issue of *Le Chat Noir*, for example, may have been an ironic self-promotion. 'Finally,' it begins, 'lovers of gay music will be able to indulge themselves to their hearts' content':

The indefatigable *Erik-Satie*, the sphinx-man, the composer with a head of wood, announces the appearance of a new musical work of which, from henceforth, he speaks most highly. It is a suite of melodies conceived in the mystico-liturgical genre that the author idolizes, and suggestively titled *Ogives*. We wish Erik-Satie [*sic*] a success similar to that previously obtained with his *Third Gymnopédie*, currently under every piano.[31]

Similarly sardonic promotions of Satie and his works appeared in *La Lanterne japonaise,* the journal of the Divan japonais, published between October 1888 and April 1889.[32] Most of these brief commentaries, including one crediting the miracle cure of a nose polyp to a hearing of the *Ogives* and a 'few applications' of the Third *Gymnopédie*, were signed by one 'Virginie Lebeau' – a pseudonym, many speculate, for the composer himself.[33] Whether or not he contributed to these journals, there can be no doubt that by the early 1890s Satie was steeped in hedonistic cabaret culture, and on the verge of establishing himself as one of Montmartre's chief provocateurs.

3

Parcier

With musicians, things are different . . . they are often attracted to
absurdity.
Satie

In the early 1890s, having quickly run through the funds his father
had provided, Satie sold most of his furniture and relocated to a
smaller flat at the summit of Montmartre, near the construction
site where the Basilica of Sacré-Coeur was being erected, on the
rue Cortot. He joked about his reduced circumstances, making
the exaggerated claim that the new apartment offered both an
unobstructed view to the Belgian frontier and a perch above the
reach of his creditors.[1] While changing house Satie also established
a new home-away-from-home, defecting from the Chat Noir in the
wake of an argument with Salis to become a patron and employee
of a competing cabaret, the nearby Auberge du Clou. With a
pseudo-Norman décor, the Clou attracted a clientele that was a mix
of local families and bohemian artists, and when the owners opened
a *cabaret artistique* in the basement in 1891 Satie was brought on as
a hired pianist, in part to accompany shadow-puppet productions.
The director of the shadow-theatre at the Clou was the Catalan
artist Miguel Utrillo and his shows drew a group of his compatriots
to the cabaret, including Ramón Casas, Santiago Rusiñol and
Enrique Clarassó, all of whom were central figures in the Barcelona-
based *modernismo* movement. They welcomed Satie into their circle

and were drawn to his 'artistic tactics', which Rusiñol likened to those of one of their idols, Pierre Puvis de Chavannes. Writing in the Barcelona daily newspaper *La Vanguardia*, to which all members of the group contributed dispatches, Rusiñol commented that Satie

> directs his efforts towards realizing in music what Puvis de Chavannes has achieved in painting, that is, to simplify his art in order to raise it to the ultimate expression of plainness and economy, to say in a few words what a Spanish orator would not express in elegant periods, and to envelop his musical work in a certain sober indefiniteness that would allow the listener to follow inwardly according to the state of the soul, the path traced out for him, a straight path carpeted with harmony and full of feeling.[2]

This was no faint praise; Rusiñol studied with Puvis at the Société de la Palette and considered his teacher to be the 'most universal genius of our time' as well as a 'great artist and thinker'. Puvis was an inspiration on multiple levels, not least for his maverick decision to cut ties with the Parisian art establishment after achieving success within it; having exhibited at the official Salon since 1859, he resigned twice (in 1872 and 1881) before breaking entirely to help found the Société Nationale des Beaux-Arts in 1890. He made his first mark as an artist in a series of public mural projects, including commissions for the Panthéon and Hôtel de Ville in Paris, producing works that were conservative in subject matter but radical in style. Often depicting images and themes familiar from classical art, Puvis rendered his visions of the ancient world with newly flattened perspectives, an extreme simplification of form, and a muted and often pastel palette. Progressive artists admired the heightened reality and mystical quality of these works, which they deemed essentially modern; Stéphane Mallarmé, for one, perceived the sense of anxiety in Puvis' neoclassical and

Pierre Puvis de Chavannes, *Young Girls by the Sea*, 1879, oil on canvas. Musée d'Orsay, Paris.

pastoral allegories, acclaiming him in a sonnet of homage for 'leading his time' in solitude toward an artistic awakening.[3]

Simplification, plainness, economy of means: according to Rusiñol these were the qualities in Puvis' work that Satie aimed to emulate. Equally important, however, was the thematic connection, as Puvis' updates of the classical world were a touchstone for Satie, who had all along been mining the past as a way of moving art forward. Rusiñol and his circle dubbed Satie their 'Greek musician', and described his compositions as 'baptized . . . with the name "Greek harmony"', but exactly what constituted this 'Greekness' in Satie's music has been a matter of speculation.[4] The title of the *Gymnopédies*, as we have seen, surely reflects some degree of engagement with the classical world on Satie's part. On a more technical level, a number of scholars have proposed that in the

1890s Satie was actually experimenting with the ancient modes of Greek music, offering as evidence a sketch in one of the composer's notebooks in which he laid out a series of pitches that can be manipulated to approximate a Greek chromatic scale. If this scale was indeed the fruit of research rather than independent invention, its source would not be difficult to imagine: in the course of his regular visits to the Bibliothèque Nationale Satie could well have drawn the material either directly from discussions of ancient music or from a more recent reference book, F.-A. Gevart's *Histoire et théorie de la musique de l'antiquité*, which was published in Paris in 1875.[5] Whatever its origin, the pseudo-Greek scale provided Satie with an underpinning for a number of works in this phase of his career, helping to define his identity as a backward-glancing modernist much in the vein of Puvis de Chavannes.

Although Rusiñol and his confrères may have viewed Satie as their 'Greek musician', none of them aimed to capture this association in depictions of the composer. Instead their paintings and drawings show him in the course of everyday life, at home and in Montmartre's cabarets. A painting by Rusiñol, done in 1890, depicts a bookish Satie in the corner of his small rue Cortot room; wearing dark trousers and a jacket, as well as pince-nez decorated with a black ribbon, he stares into the fire, gazing away from the viewer. The space is spare and tidy, the bed neatly made, books stacked on the mantle – and Satie's involvement with the visual arts is signalled by the collection of posters and drawings affixed to the wall. A painting by Casas from the following year shows Satie in full Bohemian regalia in front of the Moulin de la Galette; a Rusiñol drawing from about the same time has Satie playing the harmonium at the Chat Noir, top hat in place and cigarette dangling from his lips (see page 32). As a group, these portraits suggest the dual facets of the Montmartre musician: isolated and contemplative on the one hand, public and performative on the other.

Ramón Casas, *El Bohemio* ('Portrait of Erik Satie'), 1891, oil on canvas, Charles Deering McCormick Library, Northwestern University, Evanston, Illinois.

In addition, despite his close friendship with the Catalans, Satie appears to have collaborated on only a single project with any one of member of the group. For a performance of a play at Utrillo's shadow-puppet theatre at the Clou at Christmas time in 1891 he composed a brief work called *Noël*, on a libretto by popular chansonnier Vincent Hyspa, who had provided the poem for Debussy's setting of 'La Belle au bois dormant' in 1890.[6] Nothing remains of the production of *Noël*, but other music from that year documents a major shift in Satie's life and career, reflecting his brief but intense engagement with the bizarre Rosicrucian sect of Joséphin Péladan.

Péladan (1858–1918) began his career as an art critic, but in the summer of 1882 started work on a sprawling mystical-erotic novel entitled *La Décadence latine*, which eventually encompassed 26 volumes and consumed his energies for nearly a quarter of a century. In the early phases of this project, at the end of 1887, he and poet Stanislas de Guaïta founded a cult they called the Rose+Croix kabbalistique, intended ostensibly as a modern version of the secret society that traced its roots to medieval Germany. Overseen by a 'ruling council' that met in the dining room at the Auberge du Clou, the group proved above all to be a powerful vehicle for Péladan's self-promotion. By 1890 he had proclaimed himself 'Sâr' (the honorific assumed by kings of ancient Babylon) and was a widely recognized personality, traversing Paris dressed in priestly robes and a sheared fur hat, his beard pointy and unkempt, his hair well beyond his collar.

Ernest Hébert, *Sâr Joséphin Péladan*, 1882. Bibliothèque Nationale de France, Paris.

In May 1891 Péladan broke ties with Guaïta to found a new branch of the Rose+Croix cult: the Rose+Croix du Temple, which boasted an adjunct art society, the Rose+Croix Esthétique, designed to compete with the official Salons in Paris.[7] Péladan announced the formation of the group in his review of the Salon in May 1891, addressing himself in a mock-pietistic tone to the 'magnificent ones.' Stipulating that he intended to 'insufflate contemporary art, above all, aesthetic culture with theocratic essence', he promised to 'ruin the notion attached to facile execution, to extinguish technical dilettantism, to subordinate the arts to Art, that is to say, to return to the tradition that considers the Ideal as the sole aim of the

Carlos Schwabe, poster for the Salon Rose+Croix, 1892.

architectonic, pictorial or plastic effort.'[8] An article published in August in *Les Petites Affiches* declared that the Association de l'Ordre du Temple de la Rose+Croix had been formed with the intent to 'regenerate Art'; a subsequent front-page article in *Le Figaro* on 2 September 1891 announced the first Salon of the Rose+Croix for 10 March the following year. On that 'solemn' day, Péladan asserted, 'Paris will be able to contemplate . . . the masters of which it is unaware' and the 'Ideal will have its temple and knights', while the new 'Maccabees of Beauty' will sing a 'hymn to Beauty which is God'. The Salon, he proclaimed, would be a 'manifestation of Art against the arts, of the beautiful against the ugly, of the dream against the real, of the past against the infamous present, of tradition against the trifle!'[9]

In this manifesto Péladan included a list naming the artists he considered exemplary of Rose+Croix values, at the top of which was Puvis de Chavannes. He also announced a slate of musical soirées that would complement the Salon, with evenings dedicated to Bach, Porpora, Beethoven, Wagner and Franck. New music would feature as well: among the 'idealist composers who the Rose+Croix will bring to light', Péladan proclaimed, would be 'Erik Saties' (*sic*), who had composed 'suites harmoniques for *Le Fils des étoiles* and preludes for *Le Prince de Byzance* and for *Sâr Mérodack*, tragedy'.[10]

How had Satie become house composer to Péladan's Rose+Croix sect? In short, the association seems to have been nurtured in the Montmartre cabarets frequented by both men. An habitué of the Clou, Satie may well have attended the meetings of the original Rose+Croix kabbalistique and, in addition, Péladan was a regular at the Chat Noir, to the extent that an 1890 illustration by Fernaud Fau depicted him, easily recognizable thanks to his unconventional garb, in the procession of the notable adepts of the cabaret en route to performances in the provinces.[11] There was also common artistic ground, as Satie and Péladan shared a fascination with the past, and in particular an attraction to the Gothic world of the Catholic

Church, as well as the devotion to Puvis de Chavannes. Satie no doubt warmed to the eccentric vision of art Péladan proposed, and on a more practical level saw the potential of the association: struggling as a sometime cabaret pianist while still attempting to launch himself as a composer, he must have perceived in Péladan a champion who could garner publicity for his works as well as guarantee performances at the Rose+Croix salons. Beyond this, it seems likely that Satie was drawn to the occult and mystical aspects of Péladan's enterprise, and viewed his engagement with the group as an opportunity to explore the possibilities of translating these qualities into a new mode of musical expression. Fascinated by the medieval past from the time of his youth, he created elaborate sketches of imaginary dragons, sorcerers, knights and castles in the early 1880s, long before his association with the Sâr.

Satie's position within Péladan's splinter group was surely secured by 28 October 1891, the date on which he signed his manuscript of a brief 'leitmotif' for the tenth novel in *La Décadence latine*, entitled *Le Panthée*. A facsimile of the autograph score and an etching by Symbolist painter Fernand Khnopff were printed as a frontispiece to the novel; a pendant to Khnopff's artwork, Satie's melody is brief and angular, emphasizing the interval of the augmented fourth, presented without harmonization or barlines. The second work for Péladan, a hymn entitled 'Salut Drapeau', was to serve as incidental music for the Sâr's play *Le Prince du Byzance*, but the work was never performed with this musical component. Set in Renaissance Italy, the play masks a story of homosexual attraction under a far-fetched tale of gender confusion; Satie's music is cued to a key moment in the rambling drama, when patriotic fervour seizes the protagonists. Péladan's text at this juncture is a banal paean to Byzantium focused on its emblematic flag, and Satie seems not to have paid it much heed. Instead he continued to explore compositional directions he had already staked out: the melody is based on the same type of 'Greek' scale that had animated the *Gymnopédies*; form – as in the *Ogives*, *Sarabandes* and *Gymnopédies* – is based on the repetition of musical patterns and cells, rather than by the logic of Péladan's text; and the performance direction ('calme et doux') is entirely at odds with the effect expected at this emotional moment in the play. Satie, however, introduces a new element into this mix, harmonizing his Greek melody with a variety of chord types – major, minor and diminished – but restricting himself to a single chord structure, using only four-voiced chords in the same first-inversion form. As a result, the music has a consistent texture, with no hint of tonality or progress, and anticipates the aesthetic that Satie would later describe as stemming from boredom, which was 'mysterious and profound'.[12]

Satie's public debut as Péladan's composer came with the performance of another new work, three fanfares for trumpets and harps, entitled *Trois Sonneries de la Rose+Croix*, at the inauguration of the first Salon Rose+Croix at the Galerie Durand-Ruel on 10 March 1892. The same pieces were repeated at the formal musical soirée associated with the salon, held twelve days after the exhibition opening, which also featured the premiere of his three preludes for Péladan's 'Chaldean pastoral' play *Le Fils des étoiles*. Satie continued to advance his ideas of creating musical form based on repetition and stasis in these works, and much has been written about his explorations of Golden Section proportions and other mathematical formulae in them. Satie's use of such devices would be consistent with Rosicrucian interests in the occult and numerology, and it seems possible, if difficult to prove, that he relied on such manipulations as the basis for new musical designs.[13] But while only the most highly attuned or informed listener would have been able to discern the presence of these organizational systems, most who attended the soirée would have been capable of drawing some conclusions about Satie's Rosicrucian bona fides based on the programme itself, which was

Cover of the *Sonneries de la Rose+Croix* (1882), illustrated with a fragment from the mural *Bellum* by Pierre Puvis de Chavannes.

limited to his works and the venerable *Missa Papae Marcelli*, composed by the sixteenth-century composer Giovanni Pierluigi da Palestrina. The small booklet outlining the evening's 'ordre du spectacle' described the 'young master's' preludes for *Le Fils des étoiles* as 'admirably oriental in character', and characterized the *Sonneries* as marked by 'originality and severe style'. They would henceforth, according to the programme, be performed only when the 'Grand Master has given permission' or at 'meetings of the order'.[14] Published under Péladan's auspices on the heels of the soirée, the *Sonneries* were given a lavish treatment that affirmed their Rosicrucian pedigree: printed with a cover reproducing a detail of Puvis' mural *Bellum* in red chalk, the score linked the new 'kapellmeister' with the aesthetics of the sect's artistic icon.

Péladan's popular Rosicrucian salons and musical soirées continued until 1897, but Satie quickly stepped out. By the summer of 1892 he was engaged in non-Rosicrucian projects: in June he composed two preludes for Henri Mazel's historicizing play *Le Nazaréen* (decorating the score with his own drawing of a medieval castle) and in July he announced a forthcoming production of a three-act opera to be staged at the Grand-Théâtre de Bordeaux, entitled the *Bâtard de Tristan*, with a libretto by his Chat Noir colleague Albert Tinchant. Nothing came of this plan, nor of Satie's effort at almost the same time to gain election to the Académie des Beaux-Arts; among those protesting his candidacy was Maurice Ravel, who described Satie as 'a complete lunatic' who has 'never done anything'.[15] Satie would campaign twice more for a seat at the Académie, in 1894 and 1896, to no avail.

Satie's attraction to all these alternative expressive outlets was no doubt stimulated by infighting in the Rose+Croix sect that ended in Péladan's 'excommunication' of his primary financial backer, Comte Antoine de La Rochefoucauld. Satie sided with La Rochefoucauld in the rift and began to associate with the artists and mystics in his circle. No doubt emboldened by these new affiliations, Satie formally broke ties with Péladan in an open letter published in the widely read satirical journal *Gil Blas* on 14 August. The stilted language was pietistic, the tone pseudo-sanctimonious, but there could be no mistaking the fact that this was a statement of aesthetic independence:

> Truly it doth amaze me that I, as a poor man with thought for nothing but my Art, should be continually pursued and hailed as Initiator in music among the disciples of Master Joseph Péladan. This grieves me sorely and offends, for inasmuch as I am the pupil of anyone, Methinks this anyone can but be myself; the more so since methinks that Master Péladan, learned man as he may be, could never have disciples no more than in music than in painting or aught else besides . . . I do swear before the fathers of the Holy Catholic Church, that in this debate in no wise do I seek to injure or offend my friend Master Péladan.[16]

By swearing an oath of sincerity to the Virgin Mary, 'third person of the Divine Trinity', Satie implied his particular adherence to one of La Rochefoucauld's associates, Jules Bois.[17] Poet, playwright and novelist – the publication of his 'esoteric drama' *Les Noces du Satan* in 1890 gained him considerable notoriety – Bois presided over a Parisian cult of Isis, in which the Holy Ghost of the Trinity was replaced by the Virgin. In 1893 he founded the journal *Le Coeur*, which took its name from her symbol, a heart, and received its funding from La Rochefoucauld; published monthly until June 1895, it promised on its masthead a programme of 'esotericism, literature, science and arts'. In its pages Satie made a declaration even more audacious than his *Gil Blas* pronouncement: under the headline 'First Epistle to Catholic Artists', he announced the formation of a new church, the Eglise Métropolitaine d'Art. 'Brethren,' Satie wrote in 1893:

We live in a troubled hour, when Western society, daughter of the Apostolic Roman Catholic Church, is overcast by the shades of impiety, a thousand times more barbarous than in Pagan times, and seems about to perish . . . We have thus resolved, following the dictates of Our conscience and trusting in God's mercy, to erect in the metropolis of this Frankish nation . . . a temple worthy of the Saviour, leader and redeemer of all men; We shall make it a refuge where the Catholic faith and the Arts, which are indissolubly bound to it, shall grow and prosper, sheltered from profanity, expanding in all their purity, unsullied by the workings of evil.[18]

Thus Satie signalled his ambition to succeed Péladan as head of a mystic religious/artistic cult, presumably with La Rochefoucauld's backing and a core of adepts already in Bois' circle. Eager to promote these affiliations, Bois devoted significant space in *Le Coeur* to Satie, publishing in this same issue a facsimile score of the composer's so-

Antoine de La Rochefoucauld, *Erik Satie*, 1894, oil on wood, Bibliothèque Nationale de France, Paris.

entitled 'Sixième Gnossienne' (now known as the Second *Gnossienne*), which was dedicated to La Rochefoucauld. Satie's *Prélude pour La Porte héroïque du ciel* appeared in facsimile in the May 1894 issue of the journal, and in its final issue, published in June 1895, *Le Coeur* showcased Satie, offering the first published commentary on the composer's music and aesthetic, illustrated with a portrait by La Rochefoucauld. Written by his brother Conrad, the 'life-and-works' article painted Satie as an iconoclast, a man of 'transcendent idealism' happy to 'follow his thoughts into poverty' rather than acquiesce to commercial materialism. The portrait reinforced this idea of Satie's mysticism, presenting the composer in the up-to-date Divisionist style most fully advanced in the work of Paul Signac, who was also a contributor to the publication. Finally, this issue included a facsimile excerpt from the *Messe des pauvres*, Satie's most ambitious work to date, a mass setting in several movements for organ, children's choir and unison high and low voices. A departure from the established

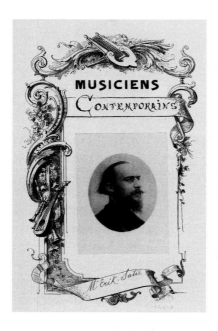

Portrait of Satie in the series *Musiciens contemporains*, 1900.

Catholic mass, Satie's work included idiosyncratic segments: in addition to the 'Prayer of the Organs' reproduced in *Le Coeur*, it featured a 'Prayer for Travellers and Sailors in Danger of Death', as well as a 'Prayer for My Soul's Salvation'. The musicians were instructed by the score to play 'in a very christian manner' and 'with great forgetfulness of the present'.

As 'Parcener and Master of the Chapel' of the Eglise Métropolitaine, Satie struck a bizarre pose clearly modelled on Péladan's affect. His arcane honorific, 'parcier', was drawn from the Anglo–Norman past, adapted from a legal term dating to the Middle Ages that connoted a joint property ownership; Satie seems to have wanted to extend the concept to the spiritual realm. While he did not style himself a Babylonian king like the Sâr, he dressed in flowing robes and sported long hair and a sharply groomed beard, and cultivated an odd persona based on a mix of bohemian cabaret humour and pseudo-religious eccentricity. He also gravitated to the written word: other than the *Messe des pauvres*, only a few small and unfinished musical works relate to his involvement with his church. What survives from this phase of his life is a trove of brochures and written pronouncements that he called 'cartularies', all issued from his *abbatiale* ('abbatial residence') – the tiny rue Cortot apartment. Linking esotericism and faux-religiosity to art and aesthetics, these documents were written in mock-Gothic script on large sheets of paper, decorated with designs and emblems of the church, penned in red and black ink. In them Satie railed against critics, including the theatre director Aurélian Lugné-Poe, who founded and managed the Théâtre de l'Oeuvre de la Fantaisie et du Songe, home to the premiere of Alfred Jarry's *Ubu Roi* in 1896, and Henry Gauthier-Villars, better known as Willy, who was the husband of the writer Colette. Willy had dismissed the *Préludes du Fils des étoiles* in a review as 'faucet salesman's music'; a furious Satie responded in an early cartulary by characterizing the critic as a 'threefold specimen of abject ignominy' and a 'mercenary of the pen'. This was just the opening salvo, following which Satie took direct aim:

Your breath stinks of lies, your mouth spreads audacity and indecency. Your depravity has caused your own downfall . . . We can but ignore the misdeeds of a clown; but We must raise Our hand to cast down the oppressors of the Church and of Art, and all those who, like you, have never known self-respect. Let those who think to triumph over Us by threats and insults know that We are resolute and have no fear.[19]

In the midst of Satie's Rosicrucian and Eglise Métropolitaine adventures, he produced a work that related to neither but conformed closely to the pseudo-religious affect of both; this was the 'Christian ballet' *Uspud*, a collaboration with Contamine de Latour, which was completed in November 1892. Described by

Latour as 'a conglomeration of every extravagance likely to astonish the public', the work related the story of the conversion of the pagan Uspud and included musical interludes scored for flutes, harps and strings. Performed as a shadow-theatre piece at the Auberge du Clou with Satie playing the harmonium, it 'roused wild approbation and violent reprobation', according to Latour, a reaction that left Satie so incensed that he became determined to see it produced at the Opéra. When the Opéra director, Eugène Bertrand, failed to respond to Satie's submission of the work, Satie challenged him to a duel, upon which a frightened and apologetic Bertrand agreed to look at the score. Satie, however, doomed the project by insisting that it be vetted by a committee of 40 musicians chosen by Latour and himself.[20] Nonetheless, for Satie, the audience with Betrand represented a significant victory, and perhaps to commemorate the occasion he published a deluxe edition of the work in 1893. *Uspud*'s printed edition included the libretto (unconventionally written entirely in lower-case letters) along with score excerpts, and featured a cover depicting Latour and Satie in profile, in the mode of a medallion. The image reflected a major development in Satie's personal life: it was created by the artist Susanne Valadon, with whom the composer had begun an affair in January that year.

Valadon, born in 1865, was a well-known figure on Montmartre, having worked as a trapeze artist, then as an artist's model for Renoir, Degas, Toulouse-Lautrec and Puvis de Chavannes, among others. A liaison with the Auberge du Clou's Miguel Utrillo resulted in the birth of a son, Maurice, in 1883, who would become a popular Montmartre artist in his own right. The Satie/Valadon affair was intense and brief, ending nastily after some six months, in June. But a letter from Satie to Valadon, written in March, attests to the affection he felt at one point for the woman he nicknamed 'Biqui':

Impossible to stop thinking about your whole being;

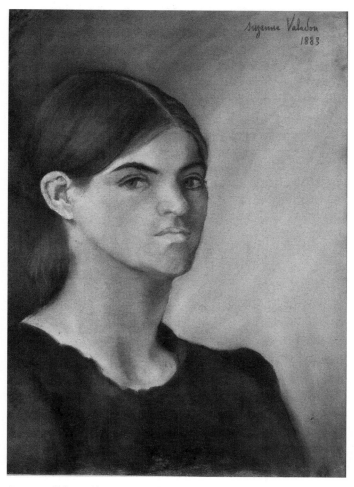

Suzanne Valadon, *Self-portrait*, 1883, crayon and pastel on paper. Musée National d'Art Moderne, Paris.

You are in Me complete; everywhere,
I see nothing but your exquisite eyes, your gentle hands, and
your little child's feet.[21]

Two compositions chart the course of the affair. The first, a cheerful song entitled 'Bonjour, Biqui, Bonjour!', is illustrated with an impromptu drawing of a girlish Valadon done by Satie. The second piece, less joyful, dates from the time of their break up, which Satie always claimed as his doing; according to his alternate stories, he either called the police on her or pushed her out of a window. The piece associated with this end-phase of the relationship is *Vexations*, a short composition for piano lasting a mere thirteen bars, which Satie indicated should be repeated a deadening 840 times. Vexing not only due to its repetitious nature and extreme length, the piece features built-in annoyances for the performer in its persistent enharmonic spellings, atonal harmonies and asymmetrical phrase structures, all of which undercut efforts to retain the music in memory. This seems to have been Satie's expressive outlet for the frustration he felt in the wake of this failed and often tempestuous affair with Valadon, which in any event was definitive: Satie had no other known romantic liaisons, and according to his friend Augustin Grass-Mick, he thereafter believed love to be simply 'a sickness of nerves'.[22]

4

Velvet Gentleman

I have long subscribed to a fashion magazine. I wear a white bonnet,
white stockings and a white waistcoat.
Satie

In 1895 Satie received a sizeable gift (7,000 francs, according to
Contamine de Latour) from his childhood friends in Honfleur,
Fernand and Louis Le Monnier.[1] He used this windfall to pay
some debts, and he invested a portion in the publication of the
increasingly elaborate cartularies of his Eglise Métropolitaine as
well as the deluxe editions of the first two *Gymnopédies*. A
considerable chunk of the money, however, went to wardrobe
improvements: Satie headed to the middle-market department
store La Belle Jardinière, where he purchased seven identical
chestnut-coloured corduroy suits with matching hats, thus
establishing the uniform he would wear for the next decade. Newly
outfitted and dubbed by friends 'the Velvet Gentleman', Satie
lived large, hosting colleagues almost nightly at one or another
Montmartre bistro. By the summer of 1896 he was broke and had
to ask his brother Conrad, a respectable chemical engineer with a
speciality in perfumes, for a loan. 'I am ruined', he wrote to 'Tiby',
invoking a childhood nickname:

> The wheel of fortune is no longer in my grasp; it is destitution . . .
> unfortunately I haven't a sou in my purse . . . It would be very
> kind if you would send Me a little help in the shape of a money

Suzanne Valadon, *Portrait of Erik Satie*, 1893, oil on canvas, private collection.

order; without which I will be exposed to cruel suffering, I tell you. After all, you may say, that serves him right; he shouldn't have spent his money so fast. I know.[2]

Even as his penned this letter Satie was facing another forced move, this time to a tiny room on the ground floor of the same building on the rue Cortot, which would cost only 20 francs per quarter. Unheated, without running water, and too small to accommodate someone standing up, this closet (or *placard*, as Satie called it) was just big enough for a bed that did triple duty, also serving as a table and as the main altar of the Eglise Métropolitaine. In light of these circumstances, it does not seem too surprising to find that Satie completed no new compositions between 1895 and

January 1897, when the Sixth (and final) *Gnossienne* was finished. Instead, he devoted himself to issuing vitriolic cartularies from his *abbatiale*, perhaps as a way of venting some of his frustrations.

The six *Gnossiennes* form an untidy group. Composed over the better part of a decade, the series begins with a piece sketched when Satie was visiting the pavilions at the 1889 Exposition Universelle and includes a core collection of three works probably composed in 1890 (and known today as *Trois Gnossiennes*), as well as a single piece from 1891, and the final work from 1897. Brief dances for piano, they suggest the Eastern influences of the Romanian ensembles Satie heard at the Exposition through their melodic use of whole-tone and other exotic scales. At the same time they rely on the slowly changing tonic, dominant and subdominant harmonies that prevailed in the *Gymnopédies*, a similarity that has led many scholars to link the two sets of dance pieces as evocations of the same classical world; typical is Alan Gillmor's view that it 'seems likely' that 'once again Ancient Greek culture was the source of Satie's rather odd title . . . the allusion being to the Cretan palace of Minos at Knossos, which had recently come very much into the news.'[3] It seems equally plausible, however, that the title relates to Satie's deepening interest in religion and occultism during this period, and particularly to his fascination with Gnosticism, which was officially re-established in France in 1890 by Jules Doinel. Founded on principles of spiritual enlighten-ment, the Gnostic church included Rosicrucianism as one of its most important orders, thus Satie's engagement with this sect would have been natural.

The *Gnossiennes* mark an important creative departure for Satie, for in these works he first begins to interweave colourful language into his musical compositions. The first *Gnossienne,* for example, combines the traditional tempo indication 'Lent' with a series of mystifying performance directives including comments such as 'very shiny', 'ask', 'with the tip of your thought' and 'postulate within yourself'. The initial humour of these remarks rests in their obvious subversion of convention, but a more complex irony may be discerned in their perverse language, which is simultaneously impenetrable and unambiguous. Prosaically vague yet poetically precise, these directives represent a major and often overlooked musical innovation, as they redraw the relationship between composer and interpreter, requiring performers to grapple with interior complexity rather than simply respond to rote technical language.

The Sixth *Gnossienne* also has the distinction of marking the end of a compositional hiatus that began in 1896 and lasted the better part of two years, during which, according to his friend Grass-Mick, Satie did 'absolutely nothing whatsoever . . . I never saw him work nor write nor take notes.'[4] Perhaps the composer was disorientated by events in his Montmartre milieu, including the death of Rodolphe Salis in 1897 and the subsequent closing of the Chat Noir. More promising for Satie in 1897 was the premiere of his *Gymnopédies* 1 and 3 in Debussy's orchestration; the performance, well received by the audience, left Satie energized and he got back to business, composing a set of six piano pieces known collectively as the *Pièces froides*, a title no doubt inspired by the winter conditions in his unheated *placard*. Grouped into two sets of three pieces, with the subtitles *Airs à faire fuir* and *Danses de travers*, these works mark another milestone in the development of Satie's technique, introducing the device of musical borrowing as a major compositional tool. Satie, it will be recalled, had incorporated a borrowed tune in his very first piece, the little *Allegro* for piano that included a snippet of the tune 'Ma Normandie'; in the *Pièce froides* the concept of borrowing takes a sophisticated turn, moving from quotation to parody. The shift occurs in the second *Air*, where Satie takes as his source material the well-known Northumbrian folk tune, *The Keel Row*. In lieu of simply quoting the jaunty melody, Satie adopted its easily recognized rhythms, then recomposed and reharmonized the melody as if to conceal the source.[5] What resulted was a new composition that audibly recalled the original tune, but at the same time presented it in a re-invented and re-arranged fashion. This fresh approach, in Roger Shattuck's phrase, left Satie 'for the first time [sounding] not medieval or Greek or Javanese, but Parisian' – in short, 'like himself'.[6] Pleased enough with his work to attempt the difficult task of its orchestration, Satie abandoned the project only after nineteen unsuccessful attempts.

The creative burst, while bright, was short-lived. In October 1898, broke once again, demoralized and in an artistic crisis, the composer rented a room in the working-class Paris suburb of Arcueil-Cachan, ten kilometres south of the city. Located in a distinctive building known as the Maison des Quatre Cheminées, his new apartment, which lacked all modern conveniences, had belonged to one of Rodolphe Salis's relatives, the colourful cabaret performer Bibi la Purée. With the help of his friends Henry Pacory and Grass-Mick, and financial assistance from Conrad, Satie moved in over time during the winter; this would be his last home and, once he was established in it, he admitted no visitors. 'No one', according to Grass-Mick, 'set foot in his room during his lifetime.'[7] Instead, Satie spent most of his time in Paris, walking to and from the city each day, stopping en route to take coffee and aperitifs and jotting musical ideas in the small sketchbooks he carried folded in his breast pocket.

Walking provided inspiration as well as exercise: Shattuck went so far as to suggest that the 'source of Satie's musical beat – the possibility of variation within repetition, the effect of boredom on the organism – may be this endless walking back and forth across the same landscape every day.'[8] Satie would start out from Arcueil each morning, stopping at the local café Chez Tulard before heading to the city. Templier reported that 'he walked slowly, taking small steps, his umbrella held tight under one arm. When talking he would stop, bend one knee a little, adjust his pince-nez and place his fist on his hip. Then he would take off once more with small, deliberate steps. This marvellous walker brought his friends "to their knees".[9] As the artist George Auriol, Satie's friend from the 1880s onward, recalled, he was fit and fearless:

> Twenty-four pairs of sturdy boots would not be an exaggeration for what such a champion of 'footing' needed. His intrepidity as a walker was so great that he made it into a pastime – and a daily one at that – to cover the distance that separates Montmartre from . . . Arcueil-Cachan . . . This 'marche bourgeoise' often took place around two in the morning, across the wild and barbarous quarters of la Glacière and la Santé where prowling 'apaches' were not unknown. This was why our musician carried a hammer in his pocket.[10]

Friends accompanying Satie on segments of these expeditions were also often surprised by his deep knowledge of French history; Pierre de Massot, for one, 'loved these long walks because Satie knew the history of old Paris right down to the last detail and his colourful monologue was entrancing.'[11] But just often Satie was alone, especially as he made his way home in the early morning (having missed the last train to Arcueil), and these hours of isolation surely had as much impact on his work as the daytime interactions in Parisian cafés.

Shortly after the move to Arcueil Satie got a more regular job, working as an accompanist for the popular chansonnier Vincent Hyspa, whom he had no doubt met earlier in the Montmartre cabarets. Hyspa, a fixture in Parisian nightlife since 1892, had performed regularly at the Chat Noir; his specialty was the *chanson parodique*, a popular genre in which well-known tunes were refitted with new texts, typically satirical, suggestive or politically provocative. Topical stories with references to current events, politics and other news provided good fodder, and scatological humour and double entendres were staples of his craft. Funny in their own right, these parodies could accrete additional levels of humour through the interplay of new words with the original text, which would be lodged in the memory of the listener, as well as through musical quotation. Since one key to the humour in these works was the disjunction between original and new material, the most widely known tunes, including folk songs, popular opera airs and children's songs, provided some of the best material for parody and were thus heard time and again in the cabarets. Other *chanson parodique* favourites were the sentimental songs and romances popularized by more sincere cabaret and café-concert performers, which were ripe for mocking. A good evening's entertainment might include a performance of such a romantic song followed immediately by a parody of it; in one characteristic juxtaposition, for example, an earnest rendition of the wistful tune 'The Lady who Passes' was followed by a satirical version, retexted to describe an accidentally swallowed prune pit – 'The Pit that Doesn't Pass.'

During his collaboration with Hyspa, Satie was involved primarily in arranging and transposing works by other composers, rather than composing new material for the singer. Only just over a quarter of the more than one hundred songs that survive in Satie's sketchbooks, which he used at the piano during performances with Hyspa, are likely to be original compositions.[12] Among these works, however, are several striking demonstrations of Satie's continuing refinement of his approaches to musical borrowing. One instance occurs in what was apparently Satie's first original cabaret song, 'Un Dîner à L'Elysée', a setting of a satirical text by Hyspa mocking reports of the French President's banquet for members of the Société des Artistes Français and the Société Nationale des Beaux-Arts. Portraying the evening as a disaster marked by bad food, dull conversation and, worst of all, a shortage of wine, Hyspa's text is marked by deft wordplay and glib irony. Likewise, Satie's music is a parody of a patriotic march, skewed by an asymmetrical phrase structure, irregular accents and a text-setting emphatic of Hyspa's satirical aims. The musical and textual punch line occurs at the end of each of the song's four stanzas, which correspond to courses in the meal, when the President brings out a military band to play the *Marseillaise*, the 'hymne vraiment français (ou française)'. Hyspa declaimed the text while Satie played a fragment of the tune itself, rendered majestically in block chords; the musical quotation delivered the ironic message of the text, mocking the very pretense of patriotically motivated support for the arts.

Satie worked a fairly busy schedule with Hyspa, performing at popular spots including the Treteau de Tabarin and the Boîte à Fursy, as well as at private parties around town. While these engagements earned him a living (if meagre), they did not satisfy his creative energies. Thus we find the composer at work on a number of fairly large-scale projects near the turn of the century, many of which were designed to allow a more thorough integration of the particular brands of humour, mysticism and medievalism that had already marked much of his literary and musical output. In tone and style these works seem to amalgamate selected influences of the cabaret and his Eglise Métropolitaine. One such project was the development of a 'clownerie' entitled *Jack-in-the-Box*, with a scenario by Jules Dépaquit, a writer, illustrator and future mayor of the 'free commune' of Montmartre. A second was the three-act play *Geneviève de Brabant*, another collaboration between Satie and Contamine de Latour, now signing himself 'Lord Cheminot'. The work was based on the old French canticle of St Geneviève, which tells the story of a young girl who is mistreated and left to die in the forest, only to be rescued by her husband before giving herself to God. The legend enjoyed widespread popularity through the nineteenth century, among other things inspiring Robert Schumann's only opera, *Genoveva* (1850), and Jacques Offenbach's opéra-bouffe *Geneviève de Brabant* (1859). More importantly for Satie and Latour, Geneviève's story occupied a prominent place in the imagination of late nineteenth-century Paris, having reached an enormous audience in the form of an illustrated broadsheet that was widely distributed at fairs and churches, as well as in popular artworks such as *images d'épinal* and woodblock prints.[13] It is hardly surprising, then, to discover that the theme of Geneviève even invaded the cabarets: in 1893 the Chat Noir mounted an elaborate shadow-puppet version of the story, complete with a musical score for fourteen singers, organ, piano and violin, by operetta composer Léopold Dauphin.[14] In short, by the late years of the century the legend had become so familiar that it was considered hackneyed, and it served as the basis for a number of parodies, including the Satie/Latour offering.

In contrast to the incidental music composed for Péladan's plays, Satie's score for *Geneviève* reflects his deep interest in Latour's text, to the extent that he drafted an abridged version of the legend alongside his musical sketches.[15] For this substantial hour-long drama, most likely also intended for shadow-theatre performance, Satie composed a prelude, three arias and three choruses; interspersed between these main numbers are two entr'actes, a hunting call and a little soldiers' march, which is played four times. All these numbers are crafted from only about ten minutes of original music, which is extended through repetition, as seven of the fifteen numbers use the same material, altered only with subtle variations. The work is scored for solo voices, chorus and keyboard, and blends Satie's two established musical styles, with the Prelude and other instrumental sections invoking cabaret idioms, while the solo airs are more in keeping with the meditative and fluid nature of the works he composed while involved with the Rosicrucian sect. While stylistically divergent, the music for *Geneviève de Brabant* shares a common harmonic sensibility: the harmonies are nominally diatonic, but inflected with elements of bitonality and chromaticism.

Considerable energy must have gone into crafting such a subtle work, but there is no evidence of any performance and Satie lost track of the composition shortly after completing it, believing that he had left the sketchbook containing the score 'on a bus'. Only after his death in 1925, when Darius Milhaud and a few other friends were cleaning out Satie's filthy apartment, did the score, which had fallen behind the piano, come to light.[16]

With no performances of either *Jack-in-the-Box* or *Geneviève de Brabant*, Satie faced another frustrating dead end. 'I'm dying of boredom', he wrote to Conrad on 7 June 1900, 'Everything I begin timidly fails with a certainty I've never known before.'[17] Still, he cut enough of a figure to be asked to contribute the essay on 'Musicians of Montmartre' for the official guidebook to the Butte that was published in connection with the Exposition Universelle in 1900, and he set an appropriately ironic tone by noting in his opening sentence that 'two or three hundred years ago, very few of the present musicians of the Butte existed, and their names were unknown to the wider (or for that matter, narrower) public'.[18] Also for the Exposition, he composed a brief piano piece entitled *Verset laïque et somptueux*, for an anthology of works by contemporary composers in which his score was reproduced in lavish facsimile, illustrated with a drawing of Paris and the Seine.[19]

The other composition of note from 1900 was yet another collaboration with Latour, this time on a three-act play entitled *La Mort de Monsieur Mouche*. Almost everything related to the project is lost, but Satie's sketches reveal something extraordinary: his music was to include ragtime syncopations. The sketches were complete months before John Philip Sousa performed syncopated American dance music in Paris in May 1900, often cited as the first occasion on which such music was heard in the city, and suggest that Satie had obtained access to sheet music versions of the latest tunes sometime earlier, probably through Gabriel Astruc, who had visited the Columbian Exposition in Chicago in 1893.[20] This would

Satie's *Verset Laïque et Somptueux*, from the series *Musiciens contemporains*, 1900.

mean that Satie was one of the first composers in Paris to begin to work with these American idioms, and that his explorations pre-dated the far more famous use of such music by Debussy in his piano piece 'Golliwog's Cakewalk' by nearly a decade.

As the century turned, Satie continued to compose light and entertaining songs, and in 1902 scored a major coup by persuading music-hall star Paulette Darty to perform his works. As Darty recalled their meeting, Satie came to her home (probably in 1902), accompanied by the music publisher Jean Bellon, 'who had an attractive voice':

> That morning I was in my bath. I heard the now-famous tune of 'Je te veux' that M. Bellon was singing, which had a special charm and such an attractive quality about it. I quickly got out of my bath to express my enchantment personally. He sat down

again at the piano and I sang 'Je te veux' for the first time. Since then I have sung these waltzes everywhere with the greatest success, and Satie has never deserted me . . . What an unforgettable man!'[21]

Indeed, for this 'Queen of the slow waltz' Satie composed some of the works that proved the most financially lucrative of his career. The number she mentions, 'Je te veux', was part of a group of waltzes he composed around the turn of the century, all of which were designed explicitly for public performance in the café-concert or music hall. This move toward popular song was a new direction for the composer, perhaps dictated by economic necessity. For 'Je te veux' Satie adapted lyrics written by his friend Henry Pacory (toning down their overt sexual references) and matched them with a lilting and fully diatonic tune; Darty's imprimatur, conveyed not only in her performances but also in sheet music stamped with her name, certainly helped to make the song a hit. Another sung waltz composed by Satie, entitled 'Tendrement', likewise served her well, but it was the 'Intermezzo américaine' entitled 'La Diva de L'Empire' that became one of her signature tunes. A cakewalk clearly based in American dance idioms, the song was extremely *au courant*; not only did it feature the latest in syncopations, but its lyrics recounted the story of a singer at the thriving Parisian music hall L'Empire, a popular spot that had been remodelled in English style in 1904. Satie shortly thereafter composed another syncopated piece for Darty, which under the title 'Le Piccadilly' seems to make a similar reference to things British. The song, however, was initially entitled 'La Transatlantique', and its lyrics describe a well-recognized type of American circulating in Parisian society around the turn of the century: the young heiress, sometimes known as 'Miss Dollar', who had come to the city in search of an aristocratic husband. Darty performed both of these works regularly, making 'La Diva' a showpiece in the revue

Devidons la Bobine and featuring 'Le Piccadilly' in the *Revue sans fiches*. Capitalizing on the Parisian fascination with all things American (and the conflation of England and America that somehow resulted) she played an instrumental role in popularizing syncopated music in Paris thanks to Satie's clever compositions. As for his awareness of these idioms, it likely resulted from his encounters not only with Astruc's sheet music, but also with Sousa's concerts on the Champs de Mars in 1900 and the performances of Les Ministrels, the 'orchestre nègre américain' at the Montmartre cabaret Le Rat Mort, which commenced in 1903.[22]

The successes with Darty did little to alleviate Satie's poverty: in 1903 he received only 70 centimes in performing rights for the year. The same year, however, saw the composition of one of his most enduring compositions, second in popular recognition only to the *Gymnopédies*: the piece entitled *Trois Morceaux en forme de poire*. Satie's decision to evoke the 'pear' in these pieces – whether visually, aurally or otherwise – sets up a joke that would have been obvious to his contemporaries, who understood the term *poire* as a slang insult meaning 'fathead' or 'fool'. This argot became widespread during the bourgeois monarchy of Louis-Philippe in the early nineteenth century, when caricaturists mocked the king by depicting his face as a pear shape, and by 1835 the association was so entrenched that even the simplest rendering of the pear could infer the anti-royalist satire of the king as fool incarnate. A second level of humour arises from the disjunction of title and musical content in the work; comprising seven pieces rather than simply the three announced 'morceaux', the music bears no apparent structural, philosophical or metaphysical relationship to the pear of the title. Finally, the title was likely intended as a joke at Debussy's expense, a retort to the older composer's condescending suggestion that Satie 'develop his sense of form', since his pieces lacked coherent structure.[23] The conductor Vladimir Golschmann later recalled Satie's account of the joke, which was perpetrated with the presentation of the score:

All I did was to write *Morceaux en forme de poire*. I brought them to Debussy, who asked, 'Why such a title?' Why? Simply, *mon cher ami*, because you cannot criticize my *Pieces in the Shape of a Pear*. If they are *en forme de poire*, they cannot be shapeless.[24]

As for content, the *Trois morceaux* are an unorthodox anthology of Satie's works from the 1890s, including newer songs and material from *Le Fils des étoiles*: of the seven movements, only the first 'morceau' is not based on earlier material. The 'morceaux' themselves form the core of the work and are framed by two opening movements ('Manière de commencement' and 'Prolongation du même') and two closing movements ('En plus' and 'Redite'). In all, the work was an extraordinary compendium of Satie's experiments and musical styles, juxtaposing lively cabaret and dance idioms with the more interiorizing and esoteric approaches of the Rosicrucian experience and the Eglise Métropolitaine. For Satie, the synthesis of such styles – of supposedly high and obviously vernacular art – made this a momentous composition. 'I am at a prestigious turning-point in the History of My life,' he wrote; 'In this work, I express my appropriate and natural astonishment. Believe me, despite the predispositions.'[25]

Alas, things did not turn as quickly as Satie had hoped. He continued to compose cabaret songs, and even wrote music for the operetta *Pousse L'amour*, on a libretto by Jean Kolb and Maurice de Feraudy, artistic director of the Comédie Royale. Performed in Paris and Nice, this was a successful work, and brought Satie some acclaim. Yet he was discouraged and in 1905, nearing 40 and describing himself as 'tired of being reproached with an ignorance I thought I must be guilty of', he enrolled for composition and counterpoint courses at the Schola Cantorum, the Parisian music academy founded in 1894 by Vincent d'Indy, Charles Bordes and Alexandre Guilmant.[26] Over the next seven years, while working by day on the chorales, fugues and other academic exercises required for his diploma, he eked out a living by night playing piano in Parisian cabarets and music halls, employment he later denounced as 'more stupid and dirty than anything'.[27]

5

Scholiste

Am I French? Of course I am . . . How do you think a man of my age
could not be French? You amaze me . . .
Satie

Satie spent a good part of the 1890s groping toward a new
compositional style, not only immersing himself in the worlds
where potential source materials abounded, but actually entering
those milieux – from cabaret and music-hall to Rosicrucian Salon –
as a creative and active participant. As a composer of both popular
songs and medievalizing melodies, he would seem to have been
especially well equipped to create music that was an amalgam of
styles, and that in addition was at once inherently modern and
identifiably French. This was a goal he shared with other composers
in France around the turn of the century, many of whom, weary
of the pervasive influence of Richard Wagner and still stinging
from the defeat of the Franco-Prussian War, were seeking cultural
vindication.

In the effort to define a new musical tradition for France,
the rediscovery of the nation's musical heritage was fundamental.
For French composers, the pre-Romantic era of Jean-Baptiste Lully,
François Couperin and Jean-Philippe Rameau provided a compelling
model, one enhanced by its distance in time and its associations
with the *ancien régime*. Access to the music of this period improved
significantly in the late nineteenth century, as the collected works
of Couperin and Rameau began to appear in modern editions in

France beginning in the 1860s, providing contemporary composers with new formal, stylistic and aesthetic resources. Dance forms of the period held a special appeal, offering an alternative to the rigid formalism and developmental orientation characteristic of the Germanic sonata and symphony. Debussy, for example, used such dance models in his first multi-movement keyboard works, including the *Petite Suite* (1888–9) and the *Suite bergamasque* (1890–1905), and Ravel turned famously in this direction with *Le Tombeau de Couperin* (1914–17). The alignment of these and similar new works with the French past was made explicit through the use of evocative titles, as well as through the implication of eighteenth-century musical forms, melodies and rhythmic gestures.

Satie, never one for the mainstream, harboured little nostalgic sentiment for the French rococo, and couched his evocations of the French past in ruthlessly satiric terms. His comment for an article in the magazine *L'Opinion*, published in 1922, is typical. 'I also want to pay homage,' he wrote, 'but Debussy is taken, so are Couperin, Rameau and Lully as well.' Instead Satie proposed that he would 'compose an homage to Clapisson', refererring to Louis Clapisson, composer of medievalizing songs and comic opera, professor of harmony at the Conservatoire from 1862 until his death in 1866, and founder of the Conservatoire's instrument museum. Those searching Satie's scores for references to this composer, or to Couperin and Rameau for that matter, will be disappointed, for Satie pressed into service a set of decidedly different – and arguably more potent – traditions. His path to this new music required a significant detour: looking for a way to 'break away from the Wagnerian adventure', and to create a 'music of our own, preferably without sauerkraut', he found himself, against Debussy's advice, back in school.[1]

Satie's institution of choice was the Schola Cantorum, founded a decade earlier to encourage comprehensive study of music and its history. In contrast to the Conservatoire, where technical skill and virtuosity were prized above all and nineteenth-century music was the focus, the Schola emphasized artistry and a broad slate of topics extending from medieval chant to contemporary music. Satie, with a career as a composer already well underway, seems to have taken the 'humble and courageous' step of returning to school as an opportunity to address gaps in his training.[2] He immersed himself in the rudiments of music, studying counterpoint with Roussel from 1905 to 1908, and taking the better part of d'Indy's famous seven-year composition course, which included work on basics such as form, analysis, sonata construction and orchestration. The programme required the completion of regular exercises, including chorale harmonizations and composition of fugues, and his note-books from the period chart his progress from simple projects to complex five- and six-voice counterpoint during his first year of study. The student who had once been singled out as the laziest in the Conservatoire now adopted the blunt view that 'there is a musical language and one must learn it', while his teacher Albert Roussel, recalling Satie's 'impeccable counterpoint', testified to his earnestness, remarking that 'his enthusiasm for Bach chorales would have singled him out even in an organ class!'[3] Not surprisingly, Satie's dedication of purpose was reflected in a new look; he aban-doned the Velvet Gentleman get-up that signalled his association with bohemians and entertainers and adopted the costume of a bourgeois functionary – a conservative three-piece suit, white shirt and tie, bowler hat and, always, an umbrella.

Study at the Schola opened a new world of contrapuntal com-position to Satie, and the successful completion of the programme – his diploma in counterpoint signed by Roussel and d'Indy was awarded with the distinction 'très bien' in 1908 – provided both credibility and a confidence boost. Exercises in chorale harmoniza-tion and fugal writing left him fluent in those forms and eager to explore the possibilities of meshing contrapuntal techniques with his own established style, marked by dissonance and infused with

Pablo Picasso,
Erik Satie, 1920,
pencil and charcoal
drawing, Musée
Picasso, Paris.

irony. For Satie, the leap from academic to compositional counterpoint was profound. Generally adhering to the formal discipline
imposed by chorale and fugue, Satie explored in his explicitly
contrapuntal compositions a full range of harmonic and melodic
expression in modern idioms, and used the works as vehicles for
his own quirky brand of humour.

His first non-academic contrapuntal composition, for example,
Aperçus désagréables, originated in 1908 as a paired chorale and
fugue; in 1912 he expanded the work by adding an opening
movement, which he titled 'Pastorale'. Satie composed the piece to
play with Debussy during the lunches that the two men had every
week during this period chez Debussy, and it includes a running
dialogue inserted between the staves, which was designed to
entertain the performers. The text associated with the 'Choral', for
example, instructs the performer of the *prima* part (presumably
Debussy, the better pianist) not to turn the page, and to 'scratch' at

certain points. Debussy, no fan of the Schola's 'vestry-scented air', was bluntly critical, disparaging Satie's fugue as a work 'in which tedium disguises itself behind wicked harmonies'; already sceptical of Satie's return to academe (he had warned his friend that at his age it would be impossible to 'shed his skin') he had somewhat mockingly dedicated his first set of *Images* to 'my old Satie, the celebrated contrapuntist'.[4] 'Here I am then,' Satie wrote to Conrad in January 1911, 'holding a certificate that gives me the title of contrapuntist':

> Proud of my knowledge, I set to work to compose. My first work of this kind is a Choral and fugue for four hands. I have often been insulted in my poor life, but never was I so despised. What on earth had I been doing with d'Indy? The things I wrote before had such charm! Such depth! And now? How boring and uninteresting![5]

Writing an autobiographical sketch for the publisher Demets a few years later, Satie took a less bitter view, describing the 'beautiful and limpid' *Aperçus* to be 'most elevated in style', adding that they 'show how the subtle composer is able to say "Before I compose a piece, I walk around it several times, accompanied by myself".'[6]

And despite the critiques, Satie followed the *Aperçus* with another work much in the same vein – *En Habit de cheval*, also for piano duet and likewise structured around choral-fugue pairings. Composed during the summer of 1911, the work consists of two miniature chorales and two titled fugues – the 'Litanical fugue' and the 'Paper fugue'. Satie considered it to be 'the result of eight years of hard work to come to a new, modern fugue', a breakthrough significant enough to merit his teacher Roussel's evaluation.[7] Roussel was pleased by the score, Satie reported to his new friend, the composer and critic Alexis Roland-Manuel: 'the whole thing entertained him. He has sided with me on this new conception of the fugue, especially the expositions. He loved its little harmonies.'[8] At the time of the work's composition Satie was still grappling with his courses in orchestration and making slow progress. His notebooks teem with reminders about elementary aspects of the craft: 'flute and trumpet blend very well', 'horn and trombone – useless' and 'with three trumpets, one can do anything'.[9] Nevertheless, no doubt heartened by Roussel's praise and the sale of the duet score to the publisher Rouart, Satie decided to attempt an orchestration of *En Habit*. Though the sketches attest to the fact that it did not come easily, this project was a milestone for Satie, marking his first successful conversion of a composition from keyboard to orchestral scoring – in this case a rather pared-down ensemble of winds, brass, and strings.

During his tenure at the Schola, Satie continued to perform in café-concert and music-hall programmes, and, in part due to the attention he gained in those venues, emerged as a presence in his suburban Arcueil-Cachan community. In 1908 he began attending meetings of its Radical-Socialist party and he contributed regular music reviews to the left-leaning newspaper *L'Avenir d'Arcueil-Cachan*, which was edited by architect Alexandre Templier, father of Satie's future biographer. He also organized concerts, known as Matinées Artistiques, for the town's Cercle Lyrique et Théâtral, calling on Hyspa, Darty and other stars of his acquaintance to perform in this series. More broadly, he was involved in founding a number of civic organizations, including a group devoted to historic preservation in Arcueil (a town that even today boasts a Roman aqueduct) and one specifically for exiles from Normandy and like-minded places – Maine, Poitou and Canada.[10] He served as 'Superintendant' of the town's Patronage laïque (a charitable organization for laymen), devoting himself largely to activities for children; he taught weekly solfège lessons and took classes of schoolchildren on regular outings. In 1909 he was given the honorific title 'Officier d'Académie' in recognition of his involvements, and that summer the locals hosted a Vin d'honneur as a commendation for his contributions. Satie's period of civic engagement, unfortunately, was short lived, brought to an end in 1910 following an argument with the organizers of the Patronage laïque. Nonetheless, for the townspeople of Arcueil Satie remained to his death a memorable and down-to-earth presence, the composer of a few well-loved popular songs and waltzes and a self-described 'old Bolshevik' legendary for his conversion to socialism after the assassination of one of the founders of the Socialist Party in France – the pacificist leader Jean Jaurès, shot in a café on 31 July 1914, on the eve of the First World War.

6

Bourgeois Radical

When I was young, people used to say to me 'Wait until you're fifty,
you'll see'. I am fifty. I haven't seen anything.
Satie

For Satie, 1911 was a breakthrough year. In January Maurice Ravel,
whom Satie had met nearly twenty years earlier at the Montmartre
cabaret La Nouvelle Athènes, showcased his music at a Salle
Gaveau concert of the newly formed Société Musicale Indépendante
(SMI). Ravel had founded the group the previous year after resign-
ing from the Société Nationale de Musique in protest and, with
Gabriel Fauré as its honorary president, the organization mounted
concerts of music by contemporary composers including Florent
Schmitt, Chares Koechlin and Maurice Delage in its inaugural
season. For the opening concert of 1911, held on 16 January, the
programme focused on Satie, and particularly on his early works:
featured were the second *Sarabande* (1887), the Prelude to Act 1 of
Le Fils des étoiles (1891) and the third *Gymnopédie* (1888), all played
by Ravel himself. An unsigned programme note offered an
appreciative assessment of the composer, positioning him for the
first (but hardly the last) time as a 'genial precursor' of modern
French music, who occupied a 'truly exceptional place in the
history of contemporary art':

On the margins of his own epoch, this isolated figure long ago
wrote several brief pages that are those of a precursor of genius.

These works, unfortunately few in number, surprise one through their prescience of modern vocabulary and through the quasi-prophetical character of certain harmonic discoveries . . . With today's performance of the Second *Sarabande* (which bears the astonishing date of 1887), Maurice Ravel will prove the esteem in which the most 'advanced' composers hold this creator who, a quarter century ago, was already speaking the audacious musical idiom of tomorrow.[1]

Suddenly Satie, who had spent more than twenty years labouring in comparative obscurity, was in the public eye. Only weeks later, in March 1911, a review of the concert by Michel Calvocoressi appeared praising Satie as an important forerunner of Debussy and Ravel, and at a concert of the Cercle musicale on 25 March Debussy conducted his own orchestral versions of two of Satie's *Gymnopédies* to rave reviews. Satie was delighted with the performance and reported the evening's 'great success' before an 'ultra-chic public' to Conrad.[2] The attention was sustained throughout the year, as articles about Satie appeared in a variety of publications. In March a large spread on the composer appeared in the newly launched *Revue musicale s.I.M.* (published by the Société Intérnationale Musicale), and included an overview by critic Jules Ecorcheville illustrated with Antoine de La Rochefoucauld's portrait of Satie, as well as the scores for a number of his works. In April Calvocoressi published another article on Satie in the journal *Musica*, and in December he included Satie with a group of forward-looking composers ranging from Chopin to Debussy in an article in the London-based *Musical Times*, which was entitled 'The Origin of To-Day's Musical Idiom'.[3]

At the same time that Satie was garnering this critical attention, a number of his works were seeing print for the first time: in 1911 alone, Rouart-Lerolle published the *Sarabandes*, *Trois morceaux en forme de poire*, and the piano duet *En Habit de cheval*. Satie's exposure was further enhanced when he began to write articles for publication in the *Revue musicale S.I.M.* (his first literary piece, the infamous 'Memoirs of an Amnesiac', appeared in 1912) and by the end of that year a group of younger composers and critics took such inspiration from his example that they proposed he be honoured as 'Prince of Musicians'. Demurring initially from this suggestion - 'these asses are completely ignorant', he insisted - he thought twice and accepted, reasoning that 'music needs a Prince' and agreeing that 'she shall have one, by God'.[4]

A burst of compositional activity between 1912 and 1916 attests to the creative stimulus this attention inspired. In these highly fruitful years, Satie turned his attention fully to the project of integrating high and low music that he had initiated with *Trois morceaux*, most importantly producing the piano works that are generally referred to as the 'humoristic piano suites'. The series began in 1912 with the *Préludes flasques (pour un chien)* and *Véritables préludes flasques (pour un chien)*, and continued in 1913 with an amazing group of six sets of pieces: *Descriptions automatiques, Embryons desséchés, Croquis et agaceries d'un gros bonhomme en bois, Chapitres tournés en tous sens, Vieux sequins et vieilles cuirasses*, and three groups of children's pieces, given the overall title *Enfantines*. The year 1914 brought three additional works, *Heures séculaires et instantanées*, and *Trois valses distinguées du précieux dégoûté*, as well as the album *Sports et divertissements*, and 1915 saw the last of these pieces, *Avant-dernières pensées*.

Often considered to be insignificant, these 'humoristic suites' are in fact path-breaking works that redraw the parameters of piano composition, and they reflect Satie's continuing negotiation of medievalizing and popularizing impulses, of esoteric and everyday musical styles. They also reveal his growing engagement with visual art. Satie insisted that 'musical evolution is always a hundred years behind pictorial evolution', and he befriended many artists (including the Catalans) while living on Montmartre;

beginning around 1911 his scores obviously reflect an awareness of trends in contemporary visual art, noticeable especially in their emphasis on graphic design.[5] An artist himself, Satie was adept at drawing and filled numerous sketchbooks and hundreds of small cards with imaginative renderings of subjects ranging from Gothic castles to clipper ships and futuristic airplanes.[6] Calligraphy was his particular fascination, and one not reserved for special occasions: letters, notes and even marginalia are carefully inked in his unusual hand. As recalled by his friend Jean Wiéner, no matter how inconsequential the calligraphic project, Satie pursued 'total perfection', even though 'it took him a good twenty minutes to write a six-line post card'.[7]

The influence of Satie's involvements with visual art is obvious in the unconventional appearance of the scores for the humoristic piano suites. All but one of the compositions are written in notation that eliminates bar lines and key signatures, and all but two are composed without time signatures. Satie had toyed with the conventions of notation from almost the start of his career (the 1886 Latour song, *Sylvie*, it may be recalled, had no bar lines), but in these suites the technique is more thoroughgoing and put to greater expressive use. In particular, freed from the conventional scaffolding of measures and metre the musical notes assume a fresh quality, and can be manipulated to great visual effect to reinforce the expressive content or meaning of a given piece. Also apparent in the humoristic suites is Satie's expansion of his experiments with language and music; no longer limited to performance directives, his commentaries take shape as epigraphs and small narratives that are inserted between the staves of music but not meant to be spoken or sung.

Satie's experiments with the integration of music and text constitute an utterly new conception of composition. From the origin of keyboard music down to his own day, words had appeared in piano scores in two basic guises: first, in titles, and second, in standardized instructions for the performer, such as 'allegro', 'largo', 'legato', and so on. In the humoristic suites, Satie expanded on both conventions, and in addition explored a variety of new possibilities, creating compositional complexes in which texts and music combined to generate expressive content that transcended a work's individual elements. Although this idea may sound familiar – bringing to mind the Wagnerian ideal of the *Gesamtkunstwerk*, or 'total work of art' – Satie's impulses and objectives could not have been further removed from those motivating Wagner. As we have seen, Satie had begun to experiment with the possibilities of using texts in his compositions as early as the 1890s, with the *Gnossiennes*, and continued these explorations right up through the composition of *En Habit de cheval* in 1911. One indisputable influence in this regard was the *fin de siècle* cabaret, where language was developing as the centrepiece of a unique mode of ironic humour that was captured in contemporary parlance by the complex term *blague*. A watchword of the bohemian counterculture, it was described by 1913 as a mix of acute observation and playful teasing:

> *Blague* is a certain taste which is peculiar to Parisians, and still more to Parisians of our generation, to disparage, to mock, to render ludicrous everything that *hommes*, and above all *prud'hommes* are in the habit of respecting and caring for; but this raillery is characterized by the fact that he who takes it up does so more in play, for a love of paradox, than in conviction: he mocks himself with his own banter, '*il blague*'.[8]

As an attitude and artistic stance, *blague* passed from the Montmartre studios housing bohemian artists at the close of the nineteenth century to the Montparnasse cafés frequented by the twentieth-century avant-garde, and through the shift Satie remained one of its definitive and unwavering exponents.

On the most immediate level, the *ton de blague* in Satie's humoristic piano works is conveyed in his enigmatic titles. Prefigured by *Trois morceaux en forme de poire* (1903), these range from the absurd *Flabby Preludes (for a dog)* to the mystifying *Dryed-out Embryos*, and are humorous because of their obfuscating language as well as their lack of functionality: disjunct from the music itself, the titles satirize the entire tradition of labelling musical compositions, either in neutrally descriptive terms, such as 'Sonata', or more allusive language, such as Robert Schumann's *Papillons*, or Claude Debussy's *Jardins sous la pluie*. More subtle humour emerges in Satie's inclusion of texts that go beyond performance directives to form brief narratives and conversational commentaries that are built into the compositional fabric. Defying categorization as either poetry or prose, these texts are astonishingly diverse and entertaining, covering everything from a wife's harangue of her husband in a department store to an erudite account of the activities of imaginary sea creatures. In form and structure, they are a mélange, juxtaposing snippets of spoken language with storytelling and personal asides. More often than not, the language is cool and objective, the tone is one of reserved banality, and the overall effect is that of a recorded observation of daily activities; Satie captures the mundane quality of even the wildest imaginings and conversely invests the everyday with an aura of fantasy. In short, his uses of text reflect his engagement with vanguard trends in visual art and literature, and attest to his continuing challenge of the boundaries of musical composition.

The text for the first of the *Embryons désséchés* is exemplary in this regard. The work as a whole, described by Satie in his manuscript as 'completely incomprehensible, even to me', takes as its central conceit the evocation of three obscure sea creatures, the holothuria, edriophthalma and podophthalma, each of which is the subject of a brief composition. Satie introduces each piece with an epigraph that describes the animal in question in original, mock-scientific and playfully inaccurate terms. His account of the holothuria, for example, presents a comically 'learned' explication of the animal's characteristics: 'Referred to by the ignorant as the 'sea cucumber'. Holothuria generally climbs on stones or blocks of rock. Like the cat, this animal purrs; it also spins a disgusting kind of silk. The action of light seems to disturb it. I observed a holothuria in Saint-Malo Bay.' The text integrated into the score takes the more familiar tone of colloquial reportage, describing a series of events in progress:

Leaving in the morning	Returning in the evening
It is raining	It is raining
The sun is in the clouds	The sun is no longer there
	As long as it never comes back

Cold enough. Good	Cold enough. Good
Little purr.	Mocking little purr.

What a pretty rock!	It was a really good rock
It is nice to be alive.	
Like a nightingale	Don't make me laugh, foamy bit
with a toothache.	You are tickling me.

I haven't any tobacco.
Luckily, I don't smoke.

It is a day in the life of the holothuria, viewed from the improbable, indeed ridiculous, standpoint of the animal itself.

Like other texts embedded in Satie's suites of 1913–14, the holothuria's story calls to mind the contemporary poetry of Guillaume Apollinaire, and particularly the so-called 'conversation poems' including *Les Fenêtres* and *Lundi, rue Christine*. Distinguished by their use of everyday language as well as their reliance on the techniques of juxtaposition and ellipsis, the overall effect of these poems is dislocation and incoherence.[9] In *Lundi, rue Christine*, for example, the reader must assemble a series of disjointed comments to create meaning, as consideration of even the opening stanzas of the poem demonstrates:

> The concierge's mother and the concierge will let everyone
>   through
> If you're a man you'll come with me tonight
> All we need is one guy to watch the main entrance
> While the other goes upstairs
> The gas burners lit
> The proprietess is consumptive
> When you've finished we'll play a game of backgammon
> An orchestra leader who has a sore throat
> When you come through Tunis we'll smoke some hashish
> That almost rhymes.[10]

While Apollinaire's poetry presents a more complicated set of conditions than Satie's commentaries, the similarities between the two texts are striking. Apollinaire's verse, for example, describes a scenario through a series of juxtapositions, much like those in Satie's text for 'Holothuria'. In Apollinaire's case, as we learn from the remainder of the poem, the setting is a crowded café and the poetic lines are fragments of ongoing discussions in the room, thus evoking both the café ambiance and conveying the details of individual conversations; using the same techniques, Satie more simply presents the imaginary world of his sea creature. Both Apollinaire and Satie rely on a colloquial tone, shifts between interior and exterior dialogue, and off-the-cuff comments seemingly directed at the reader (in Apollinaire's case, in the final quoted line, 'that almost rhymes') to emphasize the quality of immediacy in their work. Both texts, at bottom, aim to evoke some sense of mundane reality, whether the noise of the café or the imagined activities of the sea creature.

Satie's work, however, raises the additional issues of how to take account of the texts in performance: should they be read aloud for the benefit of an audience, or are they intended only for the eyes of the performer? Satie left one answer to this question in the preface to the piano suite *Heures séculaires et instantanées* (June–July 1914), imposingly warning interpreters that the composer 'forbids the text to be read out loud during the performance of the music' and noting that 'failure to conform with these instructions will cause the transgressor to incur my just indignation'. Astonishingly, despite Satie's history of ironic joking and false posturing, this admonition has been taken at face value, rather than, as he more likely intended, as simply another manifestation of the *ton de blague*.

The complex interaction of text and music in 'Holothuria', which is typical of these compositions, illuminates the matter. Carefully using music and language in tandem, Satie offers a fresh take on the sonata, thus tweaking one of the most venerable musical forms in the repertory. On the large scale, his mechanisms are simple: the opening section of the sonata, known as the exposition and generally characterized by the presentation of two themes in contrasting keys, is matched to the first section of the text, which describes the daylight hours. The central part of the sonata, known as the development and typically the area in which the themes are manipulated, coordinates with the textual aside 'It is good to be alive/Like a nightingale with a toothache.' The last major section in sonata form, known as the recapitulation and noted for the return of the two themes, now both in the primary key area, is cued to the text that describes the evening and the holothuria's return. Finally, a brief musical coda corresponds to the concluding couplet of text.

'Holothuria' follows conventional sonata principles by presenting two distinct musical themes in the exposition, a feature emphasized through the identification of specific sections of text with each theme: the first theme is coordinated with the text from its opening through the reference to 'purring', the second with the subsequent invocation of the 'pretty rock'. As anyone familiar with sonata form would expect, these textual associations remain stable in the recapitulation, adding the weight of language to the structure of musical repetition. In short, both music and language delineate sonata form.

Satie's aim, however, is not to render, but to parody sonata form. Having established a textual and musical outline of sonata structure, he proceeds to undo each of its fundamental principles. His main target is tonal contrast: flouting time-honoured rules, Satie presents both themes of the exposition in the tonic key, c major, and he keeps his brief development section – where composers typically go farthest afield – fundamentally static. With the coda, he veers to blatant mockery by repeating a G-major chord – accentuated by the dynamic marking forte and with the additional directive 'grandiose' – then ends his piece not in the expected key of c major, but rather on that G-major dominant chord – thus leaving the listener dangling, deprived of a much-anticipated resolution.

On a more local level, Satie relies on musical borrowing to add an additional layer of humour in 'Holothuria'. In particular, he deflates the Romantic pretence of thematic ingenuity (the idea of melodic genius and inventiveness) by using a phrase lifted from the popular song 'Mon Rocher de Saint-Malo' as his second theme. Even funnier, the premise for the musical quote is established in the preface to the work, in which the 'narrator' recalls having seen a holothuria in 'Saint-Malo Bay', and when the song is quoted (in both the exposition and recapitulation) it is coordinated with a reference in Satie's text to a 'pretty rock' – which is, of course, exactly the subject of the original song. The preface, then, may be seen as a kind of cue to the musical quotation, while the

Opening of 'Sur un vaisseau', from Satie's *Descriptions automatiques* (1913).

intersection of music and text in the second theme completes the pun. 'Holothuria' concludes with a simpler and more explicit connection of music and language, as the text of the coda ('I have no tobacco') is aligned with a musical quotation of the well-known folksong of the same name.

As this brief analysis of 'Holothuria' suggests, the humour of the text/music relationship can best be appreciated by someone with access to score and text, as well as a familiarity with the musical references Satie employs. In other 'humoristic' works of the period Satie brings another element – graphic imagery – into play, using notation and articulation marking to create musical ideograms that reinforce his narratives. This graphic imagery is possible primarily because of Satie's elimination of bar lines, and typically involves an alignment of text, music and visual elements. Again, there is a parallel in the works of Apollinaire, who, following Mallarmé's example, eliminated punctuation from his work, beginning with his first major collection of verse, *Alcools* (1913). The opening piece in *Descriptions automatiques*, 'Sur un vaisseau', is exemplary of Satie's efforts in this regard. The initial gesture of the piece sets the scene on the boat, coordinating the text phrase 'drifting with the current' with a recurring four-note musical figuration that is visually analogous to a wave. Heightened by the incorporation of slurs and staccato notes, this figuration recurs through the piece as a rhythmic ostinato, creating a visual and aural metaphor for the ocean waves. Above this ostinato, each subsequent textual event is similarly coordinated with a simultaneous musical and graphic gesture. The 'small dashes of spray', for example, are represented musically by an embellished descending scale, while a 'gust of cool air' is rendered as an ascending pattern. Satie relies on musical borrowing to reinforce this imagery and create a pun on several levels by including a fragment of the well-loved song 'Maman, les p'tits bateaux' at just the moment his text comments 'the boat gives a nasty laugh'. The quotation does double duty, evoking the subject of the composition, the boat, through a simple but unexpected external reference, and also cueing up for the audience the established allusions of the song, especially its nonsensical text 'Mother do the little boats in the water have legs?', which adds an element of childlike naïvety to the work.

With *Descriptions automatiques*, then, Satie combines music, language and graphic imagery in various ways to humorous effect. In Templier's assessment, this represents the 'first example of a new form of mysticism in Satie – a kind of elusive mystery, subtly evoked in a musical atmosphere which is partly poetic, partly amused, but very moving.'[11] This work also represents his first major experiment with an aesthetic idea that was widespread and diversely manifested in the early years of the century: namely, simultaneity. A short cut through traditional discursive processes, this artistic approach aimed to capture the essence of the modern world, and especially its fundamental characteristics of novelty and change. Satie's explorations of its possibilities in music provide further evidence of the importance of the visual arts to his own aesthetic.

Far from specific in its application, 'simultaneity' was a catchword that came into use around 1910 to describe the vast and varied efforts to synthesize time, materials, form and colour in artistic works. Introduced as a term in colour theory by Michel-Eugène Chevreul as early as 1839, and taken up by Henri Bergson as a keystone of his concept of the *durée*, or the 'persistence of the present in the past', simultaneity was essential to Cubist, Futurist and Dada artists, and to poets including Mallarmé, Apollinaire and

Blaise Cendrars. Examples abound: from the 'visual lyricism' of Apollinaire's poetic ideograms to the inclusion of newspaper fragments in Cubist collage, the desire to create integrated art that transcended boundaries was a central preoccupation. For artists of the day, music was a powerful and present model, thanks to its centuries-old reliance on simultaneity, whether in the sounding of contrapuntal lines, the confluence of music and lyric, or the perception of variegated rhythmic structures (to cite but a few examples). In Satie's work, however, the expressive possibilities of simultaneity in music were expanded to new extremes, in the end resulting in his creation of a completely new kind of artform.

Surprisingly, the world of fashion and high society would prove the critical stimulus to this radical innovation. Satie – Montmartre bohemian, middle-aged student, citizen of the dingy suburb of Arcueil – would seem an unlikely posterboy for Parisian fashionability. Yet in 1913 he met the woman who would provide him entrée into the world of high style, Valentine Gross. One of the few female members of the art staff at the elite Paris fashion magazine *La Gazette du Bon Ton*, she and Satie became fast friends; by October he was referring to her as 'one of the good ones' and dedicating his children's pieces *Menus propos enfantins* to her, while, for her part, Gross was working her magazine connections on his behalf.

Satie's relationship with Gross, often underplayed in studies of the composer, was among the most durable and unusual associations of his lifetime. The two were close from the time of their meeting, which probably took place at the family home of pianist Alexis Roland-Manuel, right up to Satie's death; she was a trusted confidante and the only woman in his inner circle. An artist trained at the Ecole des Beaux-Arts, she attracted attention in 1913 when her sketches of Isadora Duncan and of Nijinsky and the Ballets Russes dancers performing in *The Rite of Spring* were exhibited at the Théâtre des Champs-Elysées during the scandalous production's run there. Artists and writers, including those associated with the *Nouvelle revue française*, later frequented the regular Wednesday afternoon gatherings she hosted in her apartment on the Ile Saint-Louis; Satie and Cocteau would meet there in 1915. Gross and Satie maintained a lively correspondence throughout their relationship, which documents the progress of his work and sheds light on their interconnected social life, but which most revealingly illuminates a unique tenderness, unmediated by irony, on Satie's part. Addressing her variously as his 'Bonne Demoiselle', 'Chère Amie délicieuse', and 'Chère grand-fille', he treated her with an affection that sometimes suggests romantic attraction but most often remains touchingly platonic, particularly following her marriage to artist Jean Hugo in 1919, at which he and Cocteau served as official witnesses. In the professional realm she provided Satie with connections and crucial assistance at times when his poverty was dire and his mental health in jeopardy, and up until his death she remained a stalwart ally.

Among the potential patrons to whom Gross introduced Satie in 1914 was the *Gazette*'s publisher, Lucien Vogel, who that year offered Satie the commission for a work on themes of fashion, which was to be titled *Sports et divertissements*. Legend holds that Vogel first offered Igor Stravinsky the project but, unable to meet the composer's fee, he turned to Satie – who when offered a smaller sum at first refused, fearing that such a large commission might be compromising. Although colourful, this scenario runs directly counter to the reality of Satie's vigilant attention to his finances, a trait evident even on the pages of the sketchbooks for *Sports et divertissements*, where the composer meticulously recorded Vogel's instalment payments on the commission. Amounting to the handsome sum of 3,000 French francs, it was the largest payoff that Satie had ever received for one of his works.

Vogel's investment funded an extraordinary and category-defying work that put simultaneity into the service of celebrating

YACHTING.

Charles Martin's design for 'Le Yachting' from *Sports et divertissements* (1914).

and cementing the relationship between music and fashion. With its mix of piano pieces, texts, graphic designs and colour illustrations, *Sports et divertissements* is a musical adaptation of the fashion magazine, complete with up-to-date illustrations depicting the latest styles. Even its title originates in the fashion milieu: the phrase 'sports et divertissements' was a widely used slogan designed to attract upmarket tourists to trendy resorts and it can be found in advertisements published in popular women's magazines from the 1910s onward. The work's twenty very brief multimedia compositions take as their subjects the pastimes of contemporary Parisian society, ranging from real sports, such as tennis and golf, to social sports, such as flirting and dancing the tango. In its format, too, the musical album is inspired by the fashion press: just as the fashion magazine relies on the simultaneous presentation of interconnected texts and images to convey its messages, so *Sports et divertissements* depends on correspondences among art forms, adding music to the established mix. Each of its subjects is represented by a title page with a small design encapsulating the topic; the reverse side of this page contains Satie's score, which

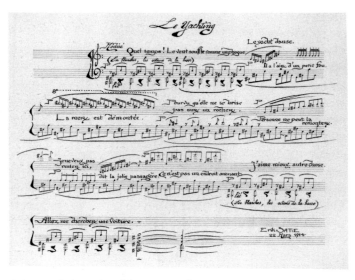

Satie, score for 'Le Yachting', from *Sports et divertissements* (1914).

combines music and texts; and the page facing the score contains a full-page colour illustration of the theme.

Sports et divertissements unquestionably adopted its design features and sophisticated tone from the *Gazette de Bon Ton*. Like Vogel's magazine, the musical album makes its first impression as a luxurious, collectible portfolio: it is oversized at approximately 430 mm (17 in) square, covered in fine paper, and backed by flyleaves in an art deco print extolling the virtues of 'love, the greatest of all games'. Produced as an unbound folio, the album opens to reveal a stylized title page featuring an icon of leisure and fashionable decadence – a modern odalisque. Satie's score appears in lavish facsimile; the musical notation is dramatic and flowing, with stylized notes in black on red staves, much in the style of some works from the Rosicrucian period. No bar lines interrupt the visual effect, and the text, in Satie's elegant calligraphy, is purposefully placed on the page so that it may be read – but not easily sung or spoken – along with the music.

Martin's illustration for 'Le Yachting', from *Sports et divertissements* (1922).

Satie's beloved *ton de blague* is evident in his preface to the
album, which is also written in careful calligraphy and reproduced
in facsimile in the score. Laden with puns, his brief text advises
readers to 'leaf through the book with a kindly and smiling finger'
and warns off deeper analysis with the admonition 'Don't look for
anything else here'. Accompanying this commentary is a brief
composition, the *Unappetizing Chorale*, which Satie notes was
composed 'in the morning, before breakfast'. His preface elaborates
on his intentions:

> For the shrivelled up and stupid I have written a serious and
>   proper chorale.
> I have put into it all I know of boredom.
> I dedicate this chorale to all those who do not like me.
> I withdraw.

Satie's use of a chorale to introduce a work devoted to fashionable themes is deliciously ironic; few genres could be more antithetical to the pursuit of stylish pastimes than this symbol of Protestant piety and music pedagogy. Informed by his intensive study of counterpoint at the Schola Cantorum, the piece is a crafty parody of the chorale tradition, modelled on a Bach chorale setting. It was not the first time the composer set himself against this towering musical figure: 'My chorales', he wrote in the preface to his earlier *Choses vues à droite et à gauche*, 'equal those of Bach with this difference: there are not so many of them and they are less pretentious.'

The score for *Sports et divertissements* is a work of art in its own right, but the illustrations seal the identification with the *Gazette*: brilliantly coloured pochoir plates, they are the work of Charles Martin, one of the magazine's most prominent artists. Commissioned to create images for the work around the same time Satie was brought into the project in 1914, Martin produced a set of illustrations to accompany Satie's music and texts. While the album was complete by summer it never went to press, however, as virtually all publishing activity in Paris came to a halt during the war. Martin served at the front, and on his return revisited the project and revised all the plates, updating them to capture the look of the new fashions of the day. The originals, after all, depicted clothing that was *au courant* in 1914 but had long since gone out of fashion, and in addition the realistic style of the drawings had become outdated. The revised plates, which make the connection between modern fashion and modern art, attest to the transformation of both clothing and modes of illustration between 1914 and 1922. More than a shift of style was at stake, however. Satie's score was not revised when the drawings were redone, and Martin's two sets of illustrations correspond with differing levels of immediacy to the events and images conveyed in the music and texts. *Sports et divertissements* thus exists in two distinct versions: in the original conception music, text and visual

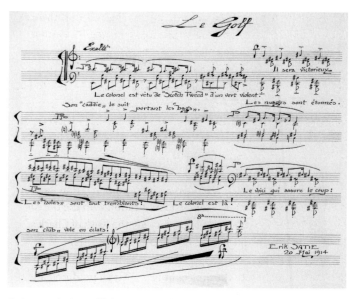

Satie, score for 'Le Golf', from *Sports et divertissements* (1914).

art are tightly integrated, while in the revised version a looser set of relationships among artforms prevails.

Consider the case of *Le Golf*. Satie's score is built around a text that recounts a surprising incident on the course:

The colonel is dressed in shocking green 'Scotch Tweed'.
He will be victorious.
His 'caddie' follows him carrying his 'bags'.
The clouds are amazed.
The 'holes' are all trembling: the colonel is here!
Now he takes his swing:
His 'club' breaks into pieces!

Long popular in Britain, golf had been introduced as a French pastime around the turn of the century and discussions of the

Illustration by Martin for 'Le Golf', from *Sports et divertissements* (1914).

sport and the clothing appropriate for afternoons on the links quickly became standard fare for fashion magazines. Martin's original drawing conveys the sense of chic that attached to the sport while faithfully portraying the details of Satie's narrative, depicting the caddy standing by with a golf bag strapped across his chest as the colonel makes his shot and shatters his club. In the original conception, then, Martin followed the model of the *Gazette's* fashion plates, illustrating the witty story suggested by Satie's composition as an up-to-date fashion scene.

By the time Martin revised the illustration, however, both the clothing and culture of golf had changed; attitudes concerning women's participation in the sport, in particular, had evolved. While female adepts of the game in 1913 were characterized by *Fémina* as a small 'passionate clan' struggling with the rudiments of the game, the fair sex took so enthusiastically to the sport that by 1921 the magazine was sponsoring an annual national tournament for women with prizes including a silver cup, cash and jewellery by

Another illustration for 'Le Golf' by Martin, from *Sports et divertissements* (1922).

Cartier.[12] Martin's revised plate for *Le Golf* takes account of these changes. While in the original illustration three well-dressed women watch passively from the sidelines as the drama of the colonel's breaking club unfolds, the later plate foregrounds a woman confidently selecting the club for her next shot as her male partner looks on. This revised illustration shows no direct connection to either Satie's music or his quirky text, but evokes in more universal terms the good life enjoyed by the upper class following the war.

The musical components of Satie's score further complicate the relationship between text and visual art. Adding a level to the illustration of the narrative, his composition explicitly represents images of the text in sonic and graphic terms. In *Le Golf*, for example, the 'trembling holes' are evoked by use of a descending chromatic scale; an ascending flourish based on unusual quartal harmonies and emphasized by a fortissimo dynamic marking provides a striking musical image of the breaking club. Satie meticulously coordinates these musical gestures to coincide with the corresponding bits of text, creating notation that provides a visual metaphor both for the shaking holes and the club breaking in the air.

Each of the twenty vignettes in *Sports et divertissements,* while lasting no more than one or two minutes, provides a rich and deeply integrated artistic experience rooted in the culture of fashion. Perhaps because of this subject matter, so often dismissed as frivolous, or because of its comic touch and the brevity of its pieces, *Sports et divertissements* is often spurned by critics. In fact, as a culminating work in Satie's series of humoristic piano pieces, it stands alone; quietly radical in its fusion of music, language and visual image, it is an unheralded achievement of musical modernism.

For Satie, *Sports et divertissements* had a practical advantage, as it eased his entrée into social circles that would prove career changing. Prime among the contacts it fostered was Jean Cocteau, the young poet, author, playwright and society figure who quickly became one of Satie's most important collaborators and champions. In addition, it served as a stimulus to works that, while less extravagant, built on its ideas: *Heures séculaires et instantanées* (June–July 1914); *Les Trois valses distinguées du précieux dégoûté* (21–23 July 1914); and *Avant-dernières pensées* (23 August–6 October 1915). It is not coincidental that each of these works was premiered in a fashionable setting.

The earliest of the pieces to debut was *Les Trois valses,* which had its first performance at the Société Lyre et Palette, a loosely organized collective of painters, writers and musicians based in the newly chic Montparnasse quarter of Paris. The list of Lyre et Palette affiliates reads like a roster of modernism: Picasso, André Derain, Henri Matisse, Jean Metzinger, Juan Gris, Amedeo Modigliani, Manuel Oritz de Zarate, André Lhote and Gino Severini all exhibited there, and Apollinaire, André Salmon, Max

Jacob, Pierre Reverdy, Blaise Cendrars and Cocteau himself read poetry. Cocteau was a regular, and it was probably at a Lyre et Palette 'Festival Erik Satie-Maurice Ravel' in 1916 that he first heard Satie's music. Reaching beyond the bohemian intellectual set, the Salle Huyghens events drew a high-society crowd; on one typical occasion, according to a newspaper report, rows of 'splendid, shining limousines' idled their engines while their well-heeled owners enjoyed a poetry reading inside.[13]

On the programme of the Satie/Ravel concert in April 1916 were performances of two new songs, 'La Statue de Bronze' and 'Daphénéo', and *Trois morceaux en forme de poire* of 1903. An important event for Satie, the concert was introduced by Roland-Manuel, who gave a background lecture on Satie's life and compositional aesthetic, and raised the composer's visibility by establishing the first chronology of his works.[14] The concert also set the stage for the more famous 'Instant Erik Satie' sponsored by the Lyre et Palette in November 1916, held in conjunction with an exhibit in which works by Kisling, Oritz, Matisse, Picasso and Modigliani were displayed alongside African masks and sculptures lent to the gallery by the dealer Paul Guillaume. At this event Satie gave the premiere performance of *Les Trois valses distinguées du précieux dégoûté,* and Cocteau and Cendrars each read a poem in the composer's honour – the wordplay-filled 'Hommage à Erik Satie' from Cocteau, and from Cendrars the punning 'Le Music Kiss Me (*Le Musickissme*)'.

The setting for the premiere of *Heures séculaires* was the Galerie Barbazanges, the art gallery overseen by top fashion designer Paul Poiret. Having begun his career as a couturier just after the turn of the century, Poiret had established himself as a major force in fashion by introducing highly unconventional garments, including dresses that required neither corseting nor bustling, hobble skirts and even harem-style pantalons for women. He also amassed not one but two of the finest art collections in Paris: the first, which he sold at auction in 1912, focused on eighteenth-century work, the second, which he began immediately thereafter, on works of his contemporaries. Also a patron of music, he showcased new music in regular concerts at the Galerie Barbazanges, often combining the presentation of musical works with the exhibition of new art. Such was the case at the famous Salon D'Antin in 1916, a blockbuster series devoted to 'Painting, Poetry, Music' sponsored by the review *SIC* (short for *Sons-Idées-Couleurs*). The programme for the Salon included an exhibition of avant-garde art, two literary matinees and two musical matinees. While a large number of paintings were on view for the first time during this show, the exhibition is famous for one in particular, Picasso's *Les Demoiselles d'Avignon*, which shocked and scandalized audiences at the opening even though it had been completed nine years earlier. The literary and musical events adjunct to this exhibition included poetry readings by poets Max Jacob and Apollinaire and concerts featuring works by Satie, Milhaud, Stravinsky and Georges Auric. The first of these musical performances included Satie's *Gymnopédies* and a *Sarabande* for piano, and Stravinsky's *Three Pieces for String Quartet*. The event drew mixed reviews, including a harshly negative assessment from Parisian socialite Misia Sert, who was in the audience. The next day she described the evening in a letter to Stravinsky as a 'nightmare for the ears and eyes' with music (including his own) that was nothing more than 'poor man's sauerkraut'.[15]

Satie's *Avant-dernières pensées* had its premiere at a less well-known but equally important art gallery-cum-fashion salon, the Galerie Thomas, run by Poiret's sister, Germaine Bongard. Almost completely unknown today, Bongard was significant enough in 1912 to merit a full-page profile in *Vogue*, and was in addition an important figure in the circle of Montparnasse modernists.[16] She made her mark by sponsoring a number of interdisciplinary artistic events at the Galerie with the assistance of her lover, artist

Amédée Ozenfant (1886–1966), who is now recognized primarily for his collaboration with Charles-Edouard Jeanneret (later known as Le Corbusier) in the development of the post-war movement known as Purism. Together they organized a series of events in the Galerie Thomas designed to showcase the latest works of Picasso, Léger, Matisse, Derain, Modigliani, Vlaminck and other modernists in their group, many of whom were also involved with the Société Lyre et Palette. Three major shows at the Galerie Thomas were mounted between December 1915 and June 1916, and, as at the Salle Huyghens, poetry readings and musical performances were linked to each exhibition. Among these musical performances was a concert devoted to the music of Satie and Enrique Granados. The event was in part a memorial tribute to Granados, who had died crossing the Atlantic when a German torpedo hit his ship, but it was also a celebration of living artists, with a printed programme featuring designs by Matisse and Picasso, and performances of Satie's most recent works by the composer himself. For Satie the evening chez Bongard marked a significant career juncture, establishing him firmly as a darling of the creative set and laying the groundwork for his entrée into the city's loftiest artistic domains. Solidifying his position in the centre of the vibrant group of artists, poets, writers and musicians who were working in the war years to recast modernism as an expressive mode that could accommodate fashionable avant-garde approaches as well as pro-French political sentiment, it augured a future that would be at once stylish and scandalous.

7

Ballets Russes

The Idea can do without art.
Satie

Shortly after their first encounters in 1915, Jean Cocteau and Erik
Satie began work on the ballet *Parade*. Their stormy partnership
would last for nearly seven years, and though the fruits of their
collaboration were few in number they were bold in intent: the duo
proposed to demonstrate that modernist art could be entertaining,
fashionable and fun. Drawing on the ephemera of everyday life,
including fashion, advertising, cinema and popular song, they
devised a brand of modernism that was casual yet cosmopolitan,
and certain to appeal to high-society patrons as well as avant-garde
provocateurs. By the close of the 1920s it was the preferred style
in France and the United States, recognized as a viable alternative
to the more hermetic and abstract varieties of modernism that
emerged at the same time. Not to everyone's taste, however,
fashionable modernism à la Cocteau and Satie had its share of
detractors, and they reacted with force on the occasion of its public
debut, which arrived with the premiere of *Parade* at the Théâtre
du Châtelet in May 1917.

Satie had been involved in an earlier Cocteau project, a French
production of Shakespeare's *Midsummer Night's Dream* planned for
the Cirque Médrano in 1915 that was intended to be a marriage of
Cubism and modern music. With costumes and décor by Albert
Gleizes and André Lhote, and a score in which Satie's music was to

be the centrepiece amid compositions by Stravinsky, Milhaud and others, it was intended, in Cocteau's words, as a 'potpourri of everything we like'.[1] The production never came to fruition and Satie alone seems to have completed his contribution; entitled *Cinq Grimaces pour 'Le Songe d'une nuit d'été'*, it was a set of five short, popularizing pieces scored for music-hall orchestra. Though unrealized, the *Dream* project pointed directly to *Parade* in its heightened awareness of the potential that the mix of 'high' and vernacular elements held for modernist art. As we have seen, this had been a preoccupation for Satie from at least the time of *Trois morceaux en forme de poire* in 1903, and existed as the kernel of an idea even in his first little *Allegro* for piano in 1884; in many of his compositions thereafter, the idealized qualities of 'serious' French art music – clarity, simplicity and structural balance, as well as learned forms and techniques – coexist with the music-hall tunes, sentimental waltzes and folksongs of the everyday Paris.

This high-low mix was present in *Sports et divertissements* but takes centre stage in *Parade*. The only new work to be offered by Sergei Diaghilev's Ballets Russes in the troupe's one wartime Paris season in 1917, the ballet had an all-star creative team: scenario was by Cocteau, choreography was by Diaghilev's new lead dancer Léonide Massine, and costumes and décor were by Picasso. The group, exhorted by Cocteau to 'be vulgar', created a ballet that was simultaneously whimsical and radical, a work that took its themes and materials from everyday life, rejecting opulence and fantasy in favour of a coarse mix of popular culture and everyday art.[2] A departure from the standard Ballets Russes fare of mythology and oriental spectacle, *Parade* was a detour into the mundane world of Parisian entertainment, deriving both its title and content from the performance sideshows known as 'parades' that were typical at French carnival celebrations and *foires*. Cocteau featured characters and acts modelled recognizably on entertainments of the day, including a Chinese conjurer, a pair of acrobats and a Little

American Girl reminiscent of early film stars; Massine's athletic choreography mimicked the magic tricks, dances and tumbling routines of the circus and even included the slapstick antics of a larger than life-sized horse, manned by two dancers. Picasso's costumes and decor transferred the angularity and distorted perspectives of Cubism to the ballet stage, most aggressively in the ten-foot-tall, three-dimensional constructions worn by the Managers appearing between the acts; and Satie's score owed as much to the cabaret as the concert hall, blending ragtime with fugue and counterpoint to offend almost the entire Ballets Russes audience, from devotees of *Schéhérazade* to fans of *The Rite of Spring*. In short, *Parade*'s popularizing stance was shocking enough to prompt an uprising in the theatre, as some members of the opening-night audience jeered the work and derided its creators as 'sales boches' ('dirty Krauts'), a particularly biting insult in France at the height of World War I. At the same time, however, the ballet's transgression of the boundaries of high art and low culture was viewed in progressive circles as a harbinger of modernism; indeed, scandal in the theatre conveyed the imprimatur of avant-gardism instantly and incontrovertibly. *Parade*'s legacy as a counter-establishment work of art was sealed after one performance, and with his collaborators Satie was guaranteed a position in the new artistic order.

The generally hostile press reviews of *Parade* ridiculed Satie's score as a grand hoax. The mainstream reaction was voiced by the music critic in the newspaper *Le Figaro*, who accused Satie of taking laborious pains to 'reproduce the burlesque effects that even a dozen fairground musicians can produce without effort'.[3] Even sympathetic critics could find nothing good to say: Jean d'Udine, for example, complained in *Le Courrier musical* that he searched in vain for something likeable in the music but could find 'nothing, nothing, nothing' in this 'bad joke'.[4] One important critic, however, took a different view. In a now famous programme note for *Parade*, published in the week before the premiere, Apollinaire heralded Satie as an 'innovative musician', a composer of 'astonishingly expressive music, so clear and simple that it seems to reflect the marvellously lucid spirit of France'. *Parade*, he proclaimed, embodied the best of the French past as well as the promise of the nation's cultural future, a fusion whose importance he signalled by invoking the contemporary political phrase *esprit nouveau* as a motto for the work as a whole.[5] In a stroke, Apollinaire thus lifted Satie to a place of importance, anointing him as a modern musical representative of the national heritage.

Study of Satie's score for *Parade* illuminates some of the ways in which the 'lucid spirit of France' and its 'vulgar' twin meet in his music. French traditions of clarity and symmetry are represented most broadly in the balanced structure of the work, in which three central thematic movements (one devoted to each of the characters) are framed by an introduction and conclusion. These outer segments, recalling the piano duets Satie composed just after leaving the Schola Cantorum, include a chorale and fugue, both updated with a new, though still tonal, language. More prominent in the musical score, however, are elements evoking the popular culture of contemporary entertainments. On the level of form, this influence is reflected in the diversity of the music and by the constant and abrupt juxtaposition of stylistically different materials; in this way Satie's score replicates the stage show of the contemporary variety theatre or music hall, which typically featured a rapidly changing series of diverse tableaux. In its details, too, the music echoes the music hall, presenting a series of short and tuneful melodies matched to simple accompaniments comprised largely of ostinato and pendulum figures. Finally, Satie's score showcases one of the primary technical tools of popular entertainment, musical parody, which, as we have seen, had featured in his work with Hyspa and emerged as an important compositional device in the humoristic suites.

Parade's kinship with fashionable music-hall culture was obvious above all in the character of the Little American Girl and Satie's score for her dance. Hollywood supplied the models for this character in the form of two young starlets who ruled the silver screen in its early days: Pearl White and Mary Pickford. White, who played the lead in the popular movie series *The Perils of Pauline*, released in 1914–15, was known for her cleverness and daring stunt work, while Pickford, dubbed 'America's Sweetheart', played the cute charmer in a string of films that included *Poor Little Rich Girl* and *Rebecca of Sunnybrook Farm*, both released in 1917. The costume for *Parade*'s Little American Girl, purchased at the last minute off the rack of a Parisian sporting-goods store, combined allusions to Pickford's childish attire, which generally involved flouncy dresses and a floppy hair bow, with the suggestion of White's 'Pauline' uniform, which typically included a wide-collared middy sailor blouse.

In Parisian music halls, imitators of Pickford and White performed under evocative names such as 'Miss Rag Time' and 'Miss Kathaya Florence, The Yankee Girl'. Cocteau's 'Girl', like her music-hall counterparts, performed a routine worthy of the screen heroines, riding a horse, jumping on a train, cranking up a Model T Ford, pedalling a bicycle, swimming, playing cowboys and Indians, snapping the shutter of a Kodak camera, dancing a ragtime, imitating Charlie Chaplin, getting seasick, almost sinking with the *Titanic* and finally relaxing at the beach. The ballerina dancing the role was required to execute an unprecedented athletic routine that included numerous cartwheels, splits and jumps, prompting one contemporary critic to note that there were 'dozens of music-hall performers who can do this sort of thing better, because they are to the impudent manner born'.[6]

In keeping with her Hollywood roots, the Little American Girl's showpiece was a ragtime dance, performed to music that seemed to come directly from the USA. Thus it seems fitting that Satie's

Sheet music for *That Mysterious Rag*, by Irving Berlin and Ted Snyder (1911).

catchy 'Steamship Ragtime' had an American core: it was a
reworking of Irving Berlin and Ted Snyder's 1911 hit song, 'That
Mysterious Rag'. One of that year's best-sellers in the US (topped
by another Berlin dance tune, 'Alexander's Ragtime Band'), 'That
Mysterious Rag' never made it to Broadway but was a centrepiece
of the vaudeville skit 'A Real Girl', which was performed at the
annual Friar's Frolic, a springtime ritual of New York society. The

song reached Paris in 1913 under the title 'Mystérious Rag' and was one of the highlights of the music-hall revue *Tais-toi, tu m'affolle*s (roughly, 'Shut up, you bother me'), which played at the Moulin Rouge through most of that year.

Exactly how or why Satie landed on 'That Mysterious Rag' as his model for the 'Steamship Ragtime' remains a mystery. He never acknowledged his use of the song and no obvious connection links the tune or lyric to the scenario enacted by the Little American Girl. Furthermore, there is no evidence to suggest that Satie attended the Moulin Rouge show or that he met Berlin prior to a reported encounter in Paris in 1922.[7] What Satie probably did know was the French score of Berlin's piece, in at least one of the four versions issued by the Salabert firm: it was published in 1913 as a piano solo, as a song with English text and piano accompaniment, and in versions for large and small orchestra.

Satie's adaptation, scored for large orchestral ensemble, is not a simple borrowing from any of these arrangements, but is instead a thorough reworking of the model that alters melodies, harmonies and overall structure while leaving the rhythms of the original song almost entirely intact – thus recalling the approach he had first explored in the *Airs à faire fuir* of the late 1890s. Reorganizing the original material, he presents it in reverse order, beginning with twenty-four bars that correspond to the original chorus, moving on to sixteen bars based on Berlin's verse, and ending with eight bars that paraphrase Berlin's introduction. In each of these sections, Satie also alters the original melodies, following a formula that turns rising passages into descending ones, stepwise patterns into skips, and repeated notes into distinct and different pitches. In combination with his advanced harmonic scheme for the piece, these melodic changes obscure the original tune, masking the model so thoroughly that Satie's use of Berlin's music escaped critical notice until 1961 – a remarkably late date, given the widespread popularity of the original song.

Satie's title, 'Steamship Ragtime', is easier to explain. Derived from the scenario for the Little American Girl's turn on stage, it refers both to the general vogue for transatlantic steamship travel, which remained a novelty through the 1920s, and more specifically to the *Titanic*, whose sinking the Girl escapes. Above all, however, the ship seems to serve as a marker of Americanism, as detailed in Cocetau's description:

> The Titanic – 'Nearer My God to Thee' – elevators . . . steamship apparatus – The *New York Herald* – dynamos – airplanes . . . palatial cinemas – the sheriff's daughter – Walt Whitman . . . cowboys with leather and goat-skin chaps – the telegraph operator from Los Angeles who marries the detective in the end . . . gramophones . . . the Brooklyn Bridge – huge automobiles of enamel and nickel . . . Nick Carter . . . the Carolinas – my room on the seventeenth floor . . . posters . . . Charlie Chaplin.

This string of ideas, painting modern America as a clanky hub of endless sound, motivated the most radical innovation of *Parade*'s score, which was the inclusion of non-musical noises. Added by Cocteau, and ranging from whistles and sirens to the pecking of a typewriter and the firing of a gun, these sounds were intended to heighten the ballet's realism; as Cocteau jotted in a note on the final copy of Satie's manuscript, 'the four-hand piano music of *Parade* is not a work in itself but is intended as a background designed to put the primary subject of sounds and scenic noises into relief.'[8] Not surprisingly, Satie objected to having his music accorded such lesser status, and at his insistence nearly all of the sounds were suppressed in the performances of 1917.

As *Parade*'s creators surely recognized, the ballet was destined to be scandalous in some conservative quarters. Ever savvy, though, Cocteau chose to depict in *Parade* specific kinds of

entertainment that enjoyed a particular vogue with members of
fashionable society who, having taken up 'slumming' during the
war, had begun to frequent lowbrow haunts like the music hall and
circus. This was the same stylish crowd that remained at the core
of the Ballets Russes's audience, and by presenting to them on the
stage of the Châtelet an 'artistic' version of the acts they enjoyed in
shadier venues, Cocteau not only allowed everyday entertainment
to 'invade art with a capital A', but also validated their role as
tastemakers. In addition, the brand of musical modernism on
display in *Parade* suited upmarket Parisian tastes: accessible,
peppered with familiar French and American tunes, amusing and,
in its own way, elegant, it provided a template for up-and-coming
composers and established a link between the growing world of
jazz and the established domains of art and ballet music. *Parade*
thus marked a turning point for the Ballets Russes, heralding a
new sensibility rooted in the sophistication of upper-class life.

    Parade had a short run in 1917. Between its premiere and its
revival in 1920, the ballet's most significant afterlife occurred on
the pages of style and fashion magazines, where articles illustrated
with drawings and photographs extolled its modernity and
originality. Since many French journals had suspended publication
during the war, some of the most fervent appreciations of *Parade*
could be found in American magazines, including *Vanity Fair*,
the culture and arts magazine founded in 1913 by the legendary
publisher Condé Nast. Only months after the work's Paris
premiere, in September 1917, the magazine published an article
about the ballet by Cocteau himself and reported that Satie,
'leader of the Futurist musicians', Picasso, 'leader of the Cubist
artists', and the 'poet' Cocteau had sparked a Parisian 'fury' with
the ballet.[9] Cocteau reserved comment on Satie's music for the
end of his essay, praising his clear and natural orchestration, his
'purest rhythms' and 'frankest melodies'. The absence of 'slurring
pedals, of all evidences of the melted and hazy' in the score,

according to Cocteau, resulted in 'the unfettering of the purest rhythms and frankest melodies'. The essay's most trenchant remarks about music, however, concern the manner in which Satie used elements of dance and other popular styles to infuse the score with a modernist sensibility and 'ambiguous charm'. In *Parade*, Cocteau asserted, 'two melodic planes are superimposed', and 'without dissonance' Satie 'seems to marry the racket of a cheap music-hall with the dreams of children, and the dreams and murmur of the ocean'.[10]

In this article Cocteau tested the ideas that would form the basis for the quirky manifesto on music he published in early 1918, entitled *Le Coq et l'arlequin*. A collection of aphorisms designed as a defence of *Parade*, this little book served above all to promote Satie, whom Cocteau claimed was spearheading a 'return to order' by composing a 'music of France for France' based in the idioms of 'the music hall, the circus [and] American Negro orchestras'. The 'Impressionist' style of Debussy and Ravel, according to Cocteau, was outdated – 'enough of clouds, waves, aquariums, water-sprites, and perfumes of the night', he claimed – and Stravinsky simply extended the Russian tradition of Mussorgsky and Rimsky-Korsakov with more aggressive rhythms. In contrast, Satie's 'music of the earth, everyday music', captured the very essence of modern life and introduced into modernist composition 'the greatest audacity – simplicity'. Satie, in Cocteau's memorable phrase, composed 'music on which one walks'.[11]

Beginning in March 1918 *Vanity Fair* expanded on these same themes in a series of essays written by and about Cocteau and Satie, presenting them as the avatars of French modernism and promoting their brand of *dernier cri* avant-gardism. Carl Van Vechten's enthusiasm was obvious in the two articles he published in that issue of the magazine, which had titles describing the composer as both 'Master of the Rigolo' and 'A French Extremist in Modern Music'. Painting Satie as an innovative visionary, Van

Les Six on the Eiffel Tower, Paris, 1921.

Vechten credited him (rightly) with using whole tone scales in his compositions 'before Debussy ever thought of doing so', and described his borrowings from popular music models as 'one of the necessary links between the music of the past and the music of the future'.[12] In 1921 Satie took centre stage in the magazine, as articles either by or about him appeared in consecutive issues between September and January; in 1922 he was featured in eight out of the twelve issues. The first two articles to appear in the magazine were by Satie himself, inaugurating a series by the composer described in a photo caption as a 'satiric clown, [a] fantastic juggler'. His ironic 'Hymn in Praise of Critics', published in September 1921, was a tirade against critics rather than a hymn in their praise;[13] 'A Lecture on The Six', which appeared the following month, formally introduced readers to Satie's circle with a handsome photograph of the stylishly attired group of young composers who followed him posed on the Eiffel Tower, solidifying their identification with Parisian chic.[14] Two more of Satie's pre-concert commentaries followed: 'A Learned Lecture on Music and Animals', in May 1922, and, in October that year, 'La Musique et les enfants', which appeared entirely, and extraordinarily, in French.[15] *Vanity Fair* also solicited two new (and more conventional) articles from Satie, including an appreciation of Igor Stravinsky, published in February 1923, and a similar piece on Claude Debussy, which for reasons unknown remained unpublished.[16] Running parallel to Satie's own commentaries throughout this period was a series of articles by *Vanity Fair*'s critics, including Paul Rosenfeld and Edmund Wilson, Jr, emphasizing the importance of Satie's popularizing aesthetic to the development of modernist music. Back in Paris, Satie's status was celebrated in an expansive concert of his works sponsored by the Société Lyre et Palette just after *Parade's* premiere, in June 1917. Organized by poet Blaise Cendrars as an homage to the composer, the evening featured the premiere of *Parade* in piano reduction, with Satie and the Russian pianist Juliette Meerovitch performing, and opened yet another phase of the composer's career.

8

En 'Smoking'

Today will be the day, monsieur.
Satie

In the wake of *Parade*'s *succès de scandale*, Satie's ties with upmarket Paris were secured. Even before the ballet's premiere, the composer had received an important commission from one of the city's most influential arts patrons, the Princesse Edmond de Polignac. Born Winnaretta Singer in Yonkers, New York, the Princesse was an heiress to the Singer Sewing Machine fortune and, although lesbian, married into one of the most venerable families in the French aristocracy. Beginning around the time of her husband's death in 1901, she defined herself as a major patron of the arts, establishing a salon frequented by a glittering constellation of artists, including Proust, Monet, Colette and Diaghilev. Music was her main passion, and during World War I she provided much-needed support to a trio of composers, commissioning pieces for her salon from Manuel de Falla, Stravinsky and Satie. The works that resulted – *El Retablo de Maese Pedro*, *Renard* and *Socrate* – mixed drama and music to new effect, helping to redraw the parameters of chamber music.

It is not clear when Satie and the Princesse first met, but by the late summer of 1916 he was invited to dinner at her luxurious home on the Avenue Henri-Martin. As the Princesse recalled the evening, Satie impressed her as: 'A man of about 52 [actually 50], neither tall nor short, very thin, with a short beard. He invariably wore pince-nez, through which one saw his kindly but rather mischievous pale blue eyes, always ready to twinkle as some humorous thought crossed his mind.'¹ She proposed a commission: a student of Greek language and culture, she wanted a setting of *The Death of Socrates* from Plato's *Phaedo*, and was willing to pay Satie two thousand francs up front, with two thousand more on delivery of the piano-vocal and orchestral scores.² Satie quickly agreed, and his first inclination was to compose a musical background for a recitation of the Dialogues in Greek by the Princesse and members of her circle. He ended with a different approach, however, setting the text in a nineteenth-century French translation, for one to four female singers. For Satie, the project was daunting; he had still not begun the piece in January 1917, when he wrote to Valentine Gross, confiding in her that he 'had the jitters about "botching" this work that I want to be white and pure like the Antique. I'm in it "completely" and don't know any more where to put myself. There's something beautiful to be done with this idea, that's for sure.'³ Two weeks later, things had come into focus, and he wrote to Gross again, this time with obvious ebullience:

> What am I doing? I'm working on the *Vie de Socrate*. I have found a beautiful translation; that of Victor Cousin. Plato is a perfect collaborator, very gentle and never troublesome. It's a dream! . . . I'm swimming in happiness. At last, I'm free, free as air, as water, as the wild sheep. Long live Plato! Long live Victor Cousin! I'm free! Very Free! What happiness!⁴

Satie had turned to *Socrate* having finished work on the four-hand piano score for *Parade* in early January; 'my role is over,' he wrote to Cocteau on New Year's Day, 'yours is beginning'.⁵ Indeed, Diaghilev, Picasso, Massine and Cocteau decamped to Rome during February and March to prepare the ballet, while Satie stayed behind to orchestrate the work, a task he completed on 8

May, just ten days before the premiere. Perhaps not surprisingly, as *Parade* came to fruition, *Socrate* languished.

Things did not improve as the summer came and went. Satie found himself involved in a lawsuit that began when critic Jean Poueigh published a negative review of *Parade* in the newspaper *Les Carnets de la semaine*. Having personally complimented Satie at the work's premiere, Poueigh (writing under the pseudonym Octave Séré) turned around and blasted this 'ballet that outrages French taste', accusing the composer of incompetence and a lack of musicality.[6] Insulted by Poueigh's hypocrisy, Satie responded with a series of vitriolic postcards, in which he characterized the critic as 'an asshole – and an unmusical asshole at that' and addressed him as 'Monsieur Fuckface . . . famous Gourd and composer for Nitwits'.[7] Since the cards could be read by (at least) the postman and Poueigh's concierge, the critic sued the composer for libel and prevailed, after a stormy trial at which Cocteau, Lhote, Severini and Gris testified on Satie's behalf. The composer, condemned to a week in prison and ordered to pay a fine of a hundred francs plus a thousand francs in damages to Poueigh, lodged an appeal and the proceedings dragged into November, resulting in a verdict in Poueigh's favour. In the end the Princesse de Polignac came to Satie's aid, loaning him the money to cover the fine and damages, and with Diaghilev's patron Misia Edwards (later Sert) she lobbied for his release. On 15 March 1918, thanks no doubt to their influence, the affair came to a close, as the court suspended Satie's sentence 'on the condition that he show good conduct and not receive any prison sentence for five years.'[8] Satie managed the good behaviour but did not pay the damages due to Poueigh; he wrote to the Princesse in October 1918 that he had 'no intention of giving one cent to the noble critic who is the cause of my judiciary ills' and instead asked for permission to use the money for living expenses, which she apparently granted.[9]

Remarkably, Satie managed to be productive during these difficult months. In July 1917, no doubt inspired by the ongoing aggravations he encountered while pursuing legal advice, he composed the *Sonatine bureaucratique*, a piano piece that spoofed one of the best-known compositions for beginning piano students – Muzio Clementi's Sonatina Op. 36, no 1. Satie's parody involves direct quotation from the original work as well as a large-scale reorganization of its thematic and harmonic materials, and the humour is heightened by his implication of a text into the score, as the music is cued to the story of a bureaucrat's day, which includes 'a neighbour's piano that plays some Clementi'. This was the last in the line of humoristic piano pieces, and Satie would compose only one further major work for the instrument, the *Nocturnes* of 1919, which, with no texts or quotation, and complex formal designs, explore vastly different aesthetic territory.

In August he returned to *Socrate* but made little progress. By the following April he was still reporting to critic Henry Prunières that 'the work is coming along . . . It's a return to classical simplicity with a modern sensibility. I owe this – very useful – return to my "Cubist" friends. Bless them!'[10] Extracts of the work may have been performed for the Princesse that spring, and noted soprano Jane Bathori, who had premiered Satie's *Trois mélodies* at the Satie-Granados concert chez Bongard in 1916, sang 'a corner of the third part' of *Socrate* at her home in June.[11] Satie's conception continued to evolve, at one point even involving a children's choir, but the first full performance at the Polignac salon in February 1919 appears to have featured Bathori alone, with Satie at the piano. A month later, on 21 March 1919, Satie was at the instrument again, this time accompanying soprano Susanne Balguerie in a performance of *Socrate* at Adrienne Monnier's Left Bank bookshop La Maison des Amis des Livres, before a crowd that included Braque and Picasso, Gide and James Joyce, Stravinsky, Poulenc and Milhaud. As one of the era's most colourful chroniclers, Maurice Sachs, recalled the evening:

We did not know at first just what was in store for us, and what amusement the serious-farcical Satie had prepared for us under the name of SOCRATES . . . in truth, there were many tears in the eyes of those who listened to the death of Socrates . . . [We] were the witnesses to this phenomenon of which one speaks so often in the arts chronicles, and which is so rare: a revelation.[12]

Sachs was not alone in perceiving something new in *Socrate*. This 'symphonic drama in three parts with voice', scored for an ensemble of winds, horn, trumpet, harp and strings, and female voice (or voices; the score suggests the involvement of up to four singers), takes for its texts three segments of the Dialogues, specifically Alcibiades' eulogy of Socrates at the banquet, a conversation between Socrates and Phaedrus on the banks of the river Ilissius, and Plato's account of the philosopher's death. In sum, these excerpts convey little in the way of narrative, instead creating a triptych of moody landscapes, stoically calm, inherently classical, ultimately tragic. Satie's music matches these sensibilities in its static rhythms, slow pulse and ostinato structures, as well as its undulating, speech-like vocal lines. Harmonies are focused on open intervals, especially the perfect fourth, and orchestration is designed to reinforce a monochromatic effect. As Francis Poulenc so aptly put it, *Socrate*, with its 'limpidity, like running water', marked the 'beginning of horizontal music that will succeed perpendicular music'.[13]

The work had its first public performance, with Bathori and Balguerie singing and André Salmon at the piano, at a concert of the Société Nationale de Musique on Valentine's Day, 1920. The audience, by this point expecting humour from Satie, profoundly misunderstood the work and laughed at the philosopher's death, while critics responded with hostility; typical of this stance was the review by Jean Marnold for the *Mercure de France*, which described the score for *Socrate* as a 'total nullity' that served as background for

Georges Braque, *Socrate*, or *Still-life with Satie's Score*, 1921, oil on panel, Musée National d'Art Moderne, Paris.

a text 'intoned in the matter of a drawing-room conversation'.[14] Not all the criticism, however, was so harsh; Satie's friend Roland-Manuel offered an alternate and more enduring view of the work in the newspaper *L'Eclair*. 'All the emotion of the admirable text', he wrote, 'was expressed with nobility, discretion, and the most perfect unity.'[15] Stravinsky, who attended the performance, reportedly exclaimed afterward that 'There is Bizet, Chabrier and Satie', presumably defining a lineage of true French art.[16] For Satie's part, he claimed to have earnest and modest aims, as he wrote to the Belgian pianist and musicologist Paul Collaer after this premiere:

> I thought I was composing a simple work, without the least idea of conflict; for I am only a humble admirer of Socrates and Plato – who look like two charming gentlemen . . . my music was badly received, which didn't surprise me; but I was surprised to see the audience laugh at Plato's text. Yes. Strange, isn't it?[17]

A different reception awaited the premiere of the orchestral version of *Socrate*. A highlight of the 'Festival Erik Satie' sponsored by Count Etienne de Beaumont and mounted at the Salle Erard on 7 June, this all-Satie programme began with a lecture by Cocteau and featured a number of other premieres, including the first performance of the *Premier Minuet* and the *Nocturnes*, both played by Ricardo Viñes, as well as the better-known *Chapitres tournés en tous sens* and the version of *Parade* for piano duet played by Satie and Germaine Tailleferre. *Le tout Paris* was on hand for the event; the Princesse de Polignac attended with many other socialites who supported the event as a 'Dame protectorice'. As the critic Pierre Leroi reported for the *Courrier musical*, there was 'considerable affluence', with a 'long line of deluxe cars' parked outside the theatre.[18]

The upmarket audience surely warmed to *Socrate* in part because of the work's affinity with a more general interest in the classical world that had taken hold in the first decades of the century. Spurred in part by a wartime cultural agenda in which France aligned itself with classical tradition, thus defining a heritage distinct from the 'barbarian' Germans, elite Parisians embraced classicism in everything from Isadora Duncan's chiton-clad dances to Paul Poiret's 'Hellenic' dresses. The fashionability of classical culture would reach a high point in 1924, with Cocteau's adaptation of *Antigone*, for which costumes were designed by Coco Chanel. For Satie, the Salle Erard concert served as at least a partial vindication, helping to rehabilitate his reputation in the aftermath of the *Parade* scandal, during which he had been accused of having German sympathies. As he wrote to Etienne de Beaumont a few days after the performance, 'Thanks to you, people finally see me as a little bit more French than they did before. My *Bochisme* is now more Parisian, and has become legendary.'[19] It also propelled him more fully into the rarefied social and artistic circles he had begun to penetrate with *Sports et divertissements* in 1914; Constantin Brancusi, for one, found inspiration in *Socrate* that led to three sculptures, entitled *Plato*, *Socrates* and *Socrates Cup*. More bizarrely, it led to a conflation of identities, in which Satie was actually viewed as the modern-day Socrates. Writing in his journal in October 1916, for example, journalist and diplomat Paul Morand noted that Satie resembled Socrates; 'his face is composed of two half moons; he scratches his goat's beard between each word', while Valentine Gross later entitled her reminiscence of the composer 'The Socrates that I Knew'.[20] Much as Satie's mixture of high and low sources had been viewed as a musical result of the mingling of art and entertainment earlier in his career, so biographical detail was perceived as corresponding to artistic practice in this new phase of Satie's life and work, and he was seen to personify the aesthetic his music promoted.

And the biographical details of these years were dramatic; *Socrate* spanned an especially intense period of change in Satie's personal life. Not only was the composer contending with the Poueigh lawsuit, but just after its long-awaited resolution in March 1918 Debussy died. Satie had cut ties with his friend of nearly three decades after Debussy criticized the score for *Parade* during rehearsals a year earlier, with what Satie described as 'painful teasing – and at a rehearsal too! Quite unbearable, anyhow!'[21] Uncharacteristically, he relented and mended the rift when Debussy was in the last stages of his illness; as he told Prunières, in April that year he had written to the older composer, 'fortunately for me, a few days before his death. Knowing that he was doomed, alas, I didn't want to remain on bad terms with him. My poor friend! What a sad end! Now people will discover that he had enormous talent. That's life!'[22] At almost the same time, on the evening of 13 March, he barely missed being hit during a German air bombardment of Paris; as he wrote to Roland-Manuel, 'The shells were terribly close to me! I thought I was done for! People were killed, but not me. A bit of luck, eh?'[23] Blaise Cendrars, who happened to be present, recalled the event as well:

On the night of the shelling, in 1918, I saw a man lying at the foot of the Obelisk, Place de la Concorde. I bent over him, thinking he was dead. It was my old friend Satie. 'What are you doing there?', I asked him. He replied, 'I know it's ridiculous and that I'm not in the shelter. But what the hell, that thing sticks up into the air and I have the feeling of being sheltered. So I'm composing a piece of music for the Obelisk.'[24]

No such piece has ever surfaced.

Only weeks later Cocteau published his little manifesto on French music, *Le Coq et l'arlequin*, which, as we have seen, elevated Satie as the avatar of modern French music. But even this publication did little to raise Satie's spirits, which hit a new low. By August, penniless and alone in Paris while most of his friends and colleagues vacationed during the summer holiday, he wrote in desperation to Valentine Gross:

I suffer too much. It seems to me that I'm cursed. This 'beggar's' life fills me with loathing. I am searching for a job, whatever tiny thing there is. I *shit* on Art: I owe to it too many 'reversals' . . . The most menial tasks would not be below me, I promise. See what you can do as soon as possible; I'm at the end of my tether and can't wait any longer. Art? It's been more than a month since I wrote a note. I don't have any ideas, and I don't want to have any. So?[25]

No employment was forthcoming, but Gross seems to have arranged for an anonymous gift to the composer, to the amount of 1000 francs. This no doubt saw him through the early months of 1919, during which he made revisions to *Parade* in anticipation of its revival in the 1920 Ballets Russes season. He also returned to composition, completing the *Nocturnes* and the *Trois petites pièces montées* for music-hall orchestra, and, surprisingly, found *Parade* taken up by artists in the Dada movement, including Tristan Tzara and Francis Picabia, who viewed the ballet as emblematic of their anti-art aims.

Satie's fortunes changed even more for the better in 1920, a banner year. The upswing began in March with the premiere of his 'furnishing' pieces for small ensemble, now widely known under the title *Musique d'ameublement*. The first of these innovative compositions, completed in 1917, had been absorbed into *Socrate*, but a second set stood alone with the subtitle 'sons industriels'. Both promoted a radical concept: as the composer indicated in notes on the (unpublished) score, he intended the work as a 'furnishing divertissement': 'Furnishing music replaces "waltzes" and "operatic fantasias" etc. Don't be confused! It's something else!! No more "false music" . . . Furnishing music completes one's property . . . it's new; it doesn't upset customs; it isn't tiring; it's French; it won't wear out; it isn't boring.'

The inspiration for such an artistic work seems to have come from artist Henri Matisse, who 'dreamed of an art without any distracting subject matter, which might be compared to a good armchair'.[26] But what it amounts to is background music, or as some have argued, even a progenitor of Muzak – music not to be listened to, music that deflates the very purpose of the expressive medium. Indeed, even more than an exploration of the possible meaning of music, the *Musique d'ameublement* was an experiment in the potential of spatial music; as Darius Milhaud, who performed the two-piano score with Satie at the premiere, later recalled, 'In order that the music might seem to come from all sides at once, we posted the clarinets in three different corners of the theatre, the pianist in the fourth, and the trombone in a box on the first floor.'[27] With forces thus arranged at Paul Poiret's Galerie Barbazanges, where an exhibition of children's art was on display, the music was premiered between the acts of a play by Max Jacob, entitled *Ruffian toujours, truand jamais*. According to Milhaud,

Satie invited the audience to 'walk around, eat and drink' and shouted at them to 'Talk, for heaven's sake! Move around! Don't listen!', but all to no avail: 'they kept quiet. They listened. The whole thing went wrong.'[28] The performance did, however, earn Satie his first notice in *Vogue* magazine – in fact, in the very first issue of French *Vogue* – where the *Musique d'ameublement* garnered a mention in a column on the latest in home decor:

Furniture music? It is music that must be played between the acts of a theatrical or musical spectacle, and which contributes, like the sets, the curtains or the furniture of the hall in creating an atmosphere. The musical motifs are repeated without stop and it is useless, says Erik Satie, to listen to them: one lives in their ambiance without paying them any attention. It's up to you to find a way to hear this *musique d'ameublement* and to devise an opinion on the topic. But that has nothing to do with the furniture we're so taken with this season. It's just an opportunity to make and hear music, the passion of the moment.[29]

Two other events in 1920 secured Satie's place in stylish Parisian circles. The first, the now legendary 'Spectacle-Concert' financed by Beaumont and presented in February at the Comédie des Champs-Elysées, featured the premiere of Milhaud's *Le Boeuf sur le toit*, as well as public premieres of Satie's *Trois petites pièces montées*, Georges Auric's 'foxtrot' *Adieu, New York!*, and Poulenc's setting of three Cocteau poems, collected under the title *Cocardes*. Then, in July, Satie gained even more credibility when he collaborated with the dancer Elise Jouhandeau (née Toulemon), better known as Caryathis, on a 'fantaisie sérieuse' entitled *La belle Excentrique*. A highly touted adept of Jacques Dalcroze and his eurhythmic school, 'Carya' was also a presence in Parisian social and cultural circles, counting Chanel among her closest friends and actor-producer Charles Dullin among her lovers. For her first major post-war performance Satie composed what he described as a 'très Parisien' tour through three decades of dance entertainment in the city. Scored for a small music-hall style orchestra, the suite included three dance movements – the 'Franco-Lunar March', subtitled '1900: Marche pour une Grande Cocotte'; the 'Waltz of the Mysterious Kiss in the Eye', or '1910: Elégance du Cirque'; and a 'High Society Cancan', described as '1920: Cancan moderne' – all linked by a 'Grand Ritournelle', which was a recycled version of his 1905 cabaret song 'Legende Californienne'. So successful was the work that it had a reprise in June 1921 at one of the most stylish venues in Paris; Paul Poiret's private garden club, called L'Oasis, with Satie himself conducting the orchestra.

While the performance chez Poiret helped boost Satie's cachet, the former Montmartre bohemian reached the pinnacle of Parisian chic in 1923, when his works were showcased at the most fashionable event of the city's social season – the annual costume ball hosted by Etienne de Beaumont and his wife Edith. Immortalized by Raymond Radiguet in the popular novel *Le Bal du Comte d'Orgel*, these parties, held at the Beaumonts' eighteenth-century mansion on the rue Duroc, tapped into the pervasive mood of over-the-top celebration that took hold in Paris after the war.[30]

Hardly simple affairs, the Beaumont balls featured lavish food, plentiful drink and entertainments that always included a series of *entrées*, during which costumed characters (who were also guests) would make dramatic entrances, acting out a theme or brief narrative. These *tableaux vivants*, often rehearsed for weeks and typically accompanied by music and dance, aimed to stun with their opulent costumes and clever wit. The Beaumont mansion was an ideal site for stylish parties, beginning with a 'great Negro fête' in August 1918 (even before the end of the war), which included a performance of Poulenc's *Rhapsodie Nègre*, as well as American jazz. The parties continued annually through the 1920s, and included a 'Bal de Jeux', where guests dressed as toys and games, and a ball where one was simply invited to come 'leaving exposed that part of one's body that one considered the most interesting'. [31]

The 1923 Beaumont fête, known as the 'Bal Baroque', took for its theme the splendours of the *ancien régime*, and for this occasion the Count arranged a spectacular reunion of the team that had created *Parade*, commissioning an *entrée* with music by Satie, scenario by Cocteau, costumes by Picasso and choreography by Massine. Since the Bal Baroque in part celebrated the inauguration of the newly restored eighteenth-century organ in the Beaumonts' music room, Satie composed a work showcasing the instrument; as he wrote to the Comtesse de Beaumont in December 1922, 'The organ isn't necessarily religious and funereal, good old instrument that it is. Just remember the gilt-painted merry-go-round.'[32] His five-movement work for the instrument, with trumpets added at the end, matched Massine's choreography and a scenario by Cocteau, which is now lost. This slight divertissement, set in the eighteenth century and based on a rococo theme, concerns the discovery of a statue by two women. Simple and direct, it begins with a March, after which follow two 'searches' that were probably acted out by the two female protagonists moving in opposite directions. The statue's discovery is announced by a trumpet blast, and the work closes with a brief theme labelled 'retreat'; scored in three voices, for organ plus trumpet, the music suggests that the statue came to life when it was found. The score is economical, lasting under four minutes, but its sections were no doubt repeated as necessary to match the action of the *entrée*.

Satie participated in a second *entrée* at the Bal Baroque: for a performance by another beautiful young Parisian socialite, Mme René Jacquemire (the daughter of couturiere Jeanne Lanvin), he composed a five-song set on texts by Léon-Paul Fargue, entitled *Ludions*. Fargue was an old friend of Satie's, the author of the text set by the composer as the song 'La Statue de bronze', which was premiered at one of the soirées held at Germaine Bongard's salon in

the spring of 1916. The songs for the Beaumont party were short
and bordered on being silly; the set takes its title from a kind of toy
popular at the time, in which small objects (often a miniature diver)
were suspended in water so that they would bob up and down. The
song group includes a 'Rat's Tune', written in 1886 by the ten-year-
old Fargue for his pet white rat, a song called 'Spleen', in which a
seemingly nostalgic poet shifts tone and longs for a 'cute but
worthless blond in this cabaret of nothingness which is our life', and
'The American Frog', where, predictably enough, animal sounds are
the basis for word-play and musical jokes. All the music was light,
entertaining and popularizing, yet had an edge; as the Comte and
Comtesse de Beaumont no doubt hoped, at the 1923 Bal Baroque
high society and modernist art met on the plane of fête.

For Satie, the Bal Baroque marked a culmination of his
achievements in rarefied Parisian social circles. As usual the move
was signalled in sartorial terms: the composer received his first
smoking jacket as a gift in 1922, and in an unprecedented move
quickly donned it and arranged a professional photograph to
document his new look.

9

Dadaiste

Work is not always as unpleasant as books maintain.
Satie

Etienne de Beaumont's involvement with Satie continued in a more
entrepreneurial mode in 1924, when he financed and organized a
series of premiere performances under the rubric 'Soirée de Paris'.
Echoing the name of Apollinaire's prewar avant-garde magazine
Soirées de Paris, this title also suggested Beaumont's desire to outdo
Diaghilev as a ballet impresario, a point reinforced by his commission
of five ballets from Léonide Massine, who at that time was alienated
from the Ballets Russes. The performances were held at the fading
Montmartre music hall La Cigale, which by the 1920s was best known
for its scandalous all-girl revues. While a number of innovative
projects, including a version of *Romeo and Juliet* by Cocteau, were
included in the series, the major work to emerge was the ballet *Les
Aventures de Mercure*, with music by Satie, scenario, sets and decor
by Picasso, and choreography by Massine – another reunion of the
Parade team, this time with Cocteau pointedly left out.

Picasso's scenario for the ballet was a satire on the many-faceted
mythological character Mercury, and it provided the slightest
pretense for the work. Lacking both a discernable plot and a clear
organizational framework, the ballet is a humorous mélange of
visual effects; costumes and decor merge together, as dancers
intermingle with wooden and wicker puppets, creating an effect
likened by Gertrude Stein to 'pure calligraphy'.[1] In Satie's view, it

Pablo Picasso, Design for the curtain for the ballet *Mercure*, or *La Musique*, 1924, tempera on canvas, Musée National d'Art Moderne, Paris.

was a 'decorative spectacle' that 'related quite simply to the music hall, without stylization, or any rapport with things artistic'.[2]

This 'purely decorative' ballet liberated Satie to write music directly for Picasso, a task he relished:

> You can imagine the marvellous contribution of Picasso, which I have attempted to translate musically. My aim has been to make music an integral part, so to speak, with the actions and gestures of the people who move about in this simple exercise. You can see poses like them in any fairground. The spectacle is related quite simply to the music hall, without stylization, or any rapport with things artistic. In other respects, I always return to the sub-title 'Poses plastiques', which I find magnificent.[3]

Amid Satie's comments about the popularizing aspects of the work, the term 'poses plastiques' stands out, suggesting a strong aesthetic tie between *Mercure* and the Beaumont Balls. Indeed, the ballet evolves by groupings, or *tableaux vivants*, in much the same way as the succession of *entrées* characterized the entertainment of the balls. In *Mercure* the 'plastic' sense is exaggerated to an extreme by Picasso's combination of traditional costumes and the cut-out constructions of bent rattan that the dancers carried around the stage. The themes of the ballet's three tableaux provide a style-inflected update of mythology, as, for example, in the second tableau, where Mercury robs the Three Graces of their ropes of pearls while they are bathing; this too is reminiscent of the balls, where mythology and history formed the basis for creative and modernizing interpretations. Satie's music further reinforces the meshing of parody and popular culture, evoking a mix of dance forms including the polka, waltz and cakewalk, as well as music hall tunes.

As with *Parade*, a scandal ensued. André Breton and Louis Aragon, founders of the new Surrealist movement, came to the performance angry at Satie: Breton was still stinging from a mock trial in 1922, presided over by Satie, condemning his efforts to convene a so-called 'Congrès de Paris' to redefine the direction of avant-garde art.[4] At the premiere, the group gathered around Breton protested against *Mercure*, yelling from the back of the hall, with Aragon reportedly shouting 'Bravo Picasso, down with Satie!' until the police arrived to eject them from the theatre.[5] This altercation sealed the ballet's already considerable artistic cachet, and in the end the *Mercure* project further enhanced Satie's visibility in stylish Parisian circles. *Vogue* covered the production in its July 1924 issue, in an article illustrated with photographs and drawings, acclaiming Beaumont as the 'Maecenas of Paris'.[6] A year earlier, in June 1923, a drawing of the composer by fashion illustrator Eduardo Benito had appeared in the magazine, accompanying a story about the adventures of a fictional Parisian named Palmyre who meets the 'good musician' Erik Satie, 'bearded and laughing like a faun', and he had turned up several times later that summer in *Vogue's* coverage of the Beaumont Bal Baroque.[7]

The year 1924 had begun with the premiere of Satie's last project for Diaghilev, which certainly promised to keep him in the centre of Parisian style. The Ballets Russes had announced a 'Grand French Festival' for the winter season in Monte Carlo, with programmes designed to link the music of the glorious French past to contemporary composition. Shortly after the war, the Ballets had made the Riviera – and specifically the Casino at Monte Carlo – its winter headquarters, the better to align itself with the fashionable Parisian set that headed south for sun and sea each January. Perhaps drawn by the same attraction, Satie made one of his very rare forays beyond Paris, travelling by train to Monte Carlo for the performances. New ballets by Poulenc and Auric would be featured, as would revivals of operas by Charles Gounod – *La Colombe, Philémon et Baucis* and *Le Médecin malgré lui* – with new recitatives by (respectively) Poulenc, Auric and Satie, and Chabrier's *Une Education manquée* with recitatives by Milhaud. All of the elements of fashion were in place: the Gounod operas, while composed in the mid-nineteenth century, harked back for their subjects to the *ancien régime*, and notably to Molière, who was also the source for Auric's ballet *Les Fâcheux*, while Poulenc's *Les Biches* was an erotically charged divertissement set in a contemporary drawing room and featuring modern-dress costumes by Marie Laurencin.

The revitalized version of *Le Médecin* had its debut on 5 January, with sets and costumes by Alexandre Benois and choreography by Bronislava Nijinska, who was still basking in the success she garnered with the Paris performances of Stravinsky's *Les Noces* the previous summer. Satie had worked on his contribution through much of the second half of 1923, carefully preparing the orchestrated recitatives for this three-act comic opera, and composing perhaps the most conventional music of his career; he wrote to Milhaud in September that he was 'working like a worker at work (a rare thing)'.[8] The performance was a success, but it led to another scandal, this time on a personal level. The critic Louis Laloy was at the centre of this drama: charged with writing the programme for Diaghilev, he neglected to acknowledge Satie but heaped praise on Auric and Poulenc. Satie later learned that Laloy had been organizing opium-smoking parties in Monte Carlo, to which the two younger composers, along with Cocteau, had been regularly invited. In the end he broke definitively with Cocteau over this, and throughout the spring published a series of articles in various publications denouncing all three artists.

In the aftermath of the Monte Carlo fiasco, Satie turned abruptly away from the French classical past and toward the Dada painters and poets, who continued to linger on the radical fringe. His connections with this group dated back almost to the arrival of Dada in Paris in January 1920, when Tristan Tzara, one of its founders, identified Cocteau, Satie and Milhaud as representatives of new art that was 'the sole expression of modern man'.[9] By November that year another central figure in the group, Francis Picabia, included the pun 'Erik is Saterik' in his journal *391*, and the following January Satie contributed two off-colour 'pensées' to its illustrated supplement, *Le Pilhaou-Thibaou*.[10] His own arguably proto-Dada work, the 'lyric comedy . . . with dance music' *Le Piège de Méduse*, composed in the midst of work on the humoristic piano pieces in 1913, finally had its premiere at the Théâtre Michel in May 1921. Satie himself wrote the scenario for this absurd theatrical piece, which seems to have its roots in the *commedia dell'arte* tradition but prefigures Dada by focusing on a bizarre cast including the Baron Médusa (Baron Jellyfish), his daughter Frisette, her would-be lover Astolfo and the servant Polycarpe, and composed twelve dances for its most compelling character –

Jonas, a monkey. Also in 1921 Satie had his first encounter with Man Ray, at an exhibition of the artist's work at the Galerie Six. As Man Ray recalled the occasion, he was lost in the crowd when 'a strange little voluble man in his fifties came over to me and led me to one of my paintings . . . With a little white beard, an old-fashioned pince-nez, black bowler hat, black overcoat and umbrella, he looked like an undertaker or an employee of some conservative bank.'[11] The two repaired to a café and then stopped off at a shop where Man Ray bought a flat iron, a box of tacks and some glue. 'Back at the gallery', Ray remembered, 'I glued a row of tacks to the smooth surface of the iron, titled it 'The Gift', and added it to the exhibition. This was my first Dada object in France.'[12] It was also the start of a friendship that would last until Satie's death.

The battle between the Surrealist and Dada factions, led, respectively, by Breton and Tzara, simmered until 1923, when Tzara organized an evening he called the Soirée du Coeur à Barbe, recalling the name of the magazine he had published briefly in 1922 as an organ for anti-Breton propaganda. On the bill would be poetry readings by Cocteau, Philippe Soupault and Paul Elouard, along with Tzara's play *Le Coeur à gaz*. Satie had contributed to the journal and Tzara asked him to organize the music for the Soirée at the Théâtre Michel, which at one point was to include Stravinsky's *Trois pièces faciles* for piano four-hands, as well as works by anti-Dadaist Georges Auric. Satie himself performed *Trois Morceaux en forme de poire* with pianist Marcelle Meyer, although by the time they took centre stage most of the audience was paying no attention, involved instead in a series of altercations that required two separate police interventions.[13] One attendee recalled that Breton hit one man with a walking stick and slapped another, while a number of others were 'roughed up' before the evening was called to a halt.[14] This, too, formed a backdrop for the protest that took place at *Mercure*'s premiere.

Man Ray, *Cadeau*,
c. 1958, replica of
1921 original, mixed-
media assemblage.

More importantly, however, the Soirée set the stage for Satie's
last major work, the ballet *Relâche*. His collaborators in this
endeavour would be Blaise Cendrars and Francis Picabia, the
work's animator would be Rolf de Maré, and the performing
troupe would be the Ballets Suédois. Satie, who had admired de
Maré's troupe from the time of its arrival in Paris in 1920, was
enthusiastic about the opportunity to work with this fresh team,
which he viewed at least in part as a replacement for Cocteau,
Diaghilev and the Ballets Russes. He had attended the Swedish
Ballet's performances, many of which featured music by Les Six,
including, in October 1923, Germaine Tailleferre's *Marchand
d'oiseaux* and Milhaud's *La Création du monde,* and had been
searching out an opportunity to work with the troupe since at least
1921, when he proposed a collaboration with artist André Derain

on a ballet to be titled *Supercinéma*. His chance came in November 1923; at work on the recitatives for *Le Medécin malgré lui*, he received a letter from de Maré inviting his involvement in a ballet with a scenario by Cendrars, who had just finished working on *La Création* with Milhaud. Cendrars was called to Rio de Janeiro shortly after Satie signed the contract, but he provided the ballet scenario as promised, along with a list of three artists he thought up to the task. Satie selected Picabia, and the artist, assured that he would have 'complete freedom' as well as a 10,000 franc advance, signed on to the project.[15]

Cendrars's scenario, entitled *Après-dîner*, was explicitly about urban night-life, viewed from a male perspective, and he indicated that it was to be 'très Parisien'. Picabia expanded the format, extending it from one to two acts and including two film interludes, one after the overture and the other at the intermission. Satie viewed the changes as 'très chic' and 'very interesting indeed', and worked through the summer and autumn of 1924 to complete the score.[16] The film segments, created by vanguard cinematographer René Clair, offered him the chance to work in this nascent medium, and inspired Satie to create the first film music composed 'frame by frame'; this was the last section of the composition to be completed, and Satie was meticulous in his coordination of musical gestures with projected images.[17] Though he was in the midst of the fallouts with Cocteau, Auric and Poulenc, he maintained his sense of humour throughout this endeavour, writing to Massot that he was 'working on *Relâche* as much as I can', having 'done' all the music himself: 'all the flats (*above all*), all the sharps (*even the daggers*), have been done entirely (*from head to foot!*) by me. All this is very odd & indicates great strength of character.'[18]

By late October the score was complete and Satie was anticipating a 'lively premiere', warning that 'the enemy – this time – will meet ours. We are mobilizing!'[19] He was not proven wrong at the work's debut, which occurred on 7 December 1924 at the

Théâtre des Champs-Elysées. The work's title, *Relâche*, was alone a provocation: translating as 'no performance', it is the French term routinely posted at theatres to indicate a dark house between shows or during vacations, and the subtitle 'Ballet instantanéiste' did little to correct the notion of an artistic void. (Ironically, the lead dancer, Jean Borlin, fell ill just at the time of the scheduled dress rehearsals, so the performance had to be postponed, and the theater for *Relâche* was actually *relâche*.) The decor and costumes were equally confrontational, ranging from a backdrop of 370 reflecting mirrors that blinded the audience, to graffiti instructing dissatisfied patrons to 'fuck off', to a finale featuring Satie and Picabia driving on stage in a Citroën 5cv.

The scenario went through a number of revisions, and the final version has not come to light, but a number of details can be gleaned from Picabia's surviving plans for the project and from photographs and first-hand accounts of the performances. The cast included a hyper-fashionable woman (Edith Bonsdorff) dressed in a glittering drop-waist dress and matching turban; a man (Jean Borlin, here presumably a war veteran) in tails and a top hat, in a wheelchair; a male chorus; and a fireman who wandered in and out of every scene, smoking and emptying a bucket of water from one pail to another. The performance began with a film clip in which Satie and Picabia, shot in slow motion, jumped up and down on the roof of the Théâtre des Champs-Elysées, then fired a cannon directly at the audience. The curtain rose to reveal the blinding mirrors, and the action began when Bonsdorff rose from a seat in the theatre to take the stage. In the first act, she was joined by Borlin, who zoomed across the stage in his motorized wheelchair, only to regain the use of his legs thanks to the power of her beauty. Celebrating in a 'Dance of the Revolving Door', the couple was joined by the eight-man chorus, each member of which rose from a seat in the audience to engage in the onstage revelry. The dance devolved into a striptease that left Bonsdorff dressed only in a rose-coloured body stocking, lifted high above the stage by the group of men.

The second act continued in the same vein. A new backdrop, designed by Picabia, was a jumble of lines and arrows, in the midst of which was a scrawl of graffiti, including the slogan 'Erik Satie is the greatest musician in the world.' In a reversal of the first act, Bonsdorff reappeared on stage, now with a wreath of orange blossoms in her hair, and after being surrounded by the men, proceeded to put her dress back on. The men then stripped down to silk tights, keeping their top hats in place, before returning to their seats in the audience. Bonsdorff gathered their clothes into a wheelbarrow, dumped them in a corner and threw her wreath to a man in the audience, who crowned a woman 'queen' of the theatre. Bonsdorff took her seat among the spectators, a white curtain fell, and a young woman appeared, miming and singing the folksong 'La Queue du chien' ('The Dog's Tail'), which had long been understood to invoke off-colour meanings.

Unlike Picabia, for whom the work seems to have provided the justification for an aggressive stance, Satie appears to have viewed the *Relâche* collaboration as his opportunity to demonstrate that the Dada aesthetic did not preclude structural organization of the musical score; his composition is tightly crafted, self-sufficient and highly logical. Nonetheless, as Satie predicted, the ballet created a major scandal and resulted in a backlash against the composer, exemplified by Roland-Manuel's scathing column in the *Revue Pleyel*, entitled 'Adieu à Satie':

Relâche marks an important date in the annals of French music. Let us thank it for proclaiming its true bankruptcy, for committing suicide so well, and for dying without beauty, doubtless so as to deter later converts from martyrdom . . . Dada waylaid Satie . . . *Relâche* is the most stupid and boring thing in the world . . . Adieu *Relâche*. Adieu Satie. Hurry away to hell, together with the love of wrong spelling and the cult of false taste, this sham classicism which is nothing other than a lack of grace, and this abominable romanticism which is misjudged as sincerity.[20]

Though the criticism – issuing even from former friends and supporters like Roland-Manuel – was harsh, the benefits of this project were many. For one thing, with *Relâche* Satie had the chance to push the boundaries of the popular music/high-art mix to further extremes. Waltzes and marches prevail, and parodies pervade the score; harking back to the techniques he perfected in the Montmartre cabarets and honed in the piano suites, Satie wove popular tunes through the ballet, altering melodies, rhythms and harmonies to humorous effect. Second, the work offered Satie the opportunity to further hone his concept of large-scale musical structure. For *Relâche*, he devised his most rigorous framework, creating an elaborate 22-part mirror structure that in a sophisticated way matched the mirrored actions of the stage action – not to mention the mirrors of the decor.[21]

Most importantly, with *Relâche* Satie made his mark as a film composer. René Clair's hilarious *Entr'acte*, now recognized as an icon of early cinema, matched an absurd narrative with a mélange of disconnected images, many of which reflect early film experiments. Beginning with a projection of distorted light dots, it segues into a cross-cut series of Parisian scenes, then focuses on the kinds of oddities easily found in the city's shops, animating them: balloon dolls are inflated and deflated, boxing gloves come to life and fight one another, wooden matches burst into flame. A ballerina, shot from below, dances on a piece of glass; Man Ray and Marcel Duchamp play chess on the roof of the Théâtre des Champs-Elysées; the ballerina is revealed to be a man with a beard, moustache and pince-nez – evoking, of course, none other than Satie. A thin plot takes shape: Borlin appears dressed in Tyrolean hunting garb and is shot accidentally by Picabia; a lengthy funeral procession follows, during which the hearse, pulled by a camel, breaks away and moves through changing scenery at an ever-accelerating pace. When it comes to rest in an open field, the coffin opens and Borlin emerges, dressed as a magician; he uses a magic wand to make the remaining members of his entourage disappear before turning it on himself, and the word fin appears onscreen. But the piece is not at an end: exploiting the possibilities of film, Borlin rips through this backdrop in slow motion and is knocked to the ground and kicked in the head by de Maré – who is obviously eager to get on with the show – after which the film rewinds, pushing him back through the backdrop and restoring the word fin. This signals the start of the ballet's second act.

Satie carefully planned the score to accompany the film, among other things laying out a detailed arrangement of the orchestral forces he would employ. Some segments of the action dictated a specific musical response: the funeral procession, for example, almost mandated a quote from Chopin's famous funeral march in the piano sonata Op.2, no. 35; the ballerina's dance suggested a waltz or similar tune. Satie meets these expectations, but deflates the conventions by altering melodies, harmonies and rhythms to convey a different sensibility, which film scholar Martin Marks has characterized as 'ironic detachment and motion without a goal'.[22] Much of the score consists of vamping ostinatos and other background patterns, all designed to subtly reflect the visual images, all repeated and juxtaposed to create the larger work. For Satie, the ultimate appeal of *Relâche* seems to have rested neither in its provocations nor in its status among avant-garde expressions, but rather in its engagement of everyday materials to create modern art. As he explained in a programme note, the music:

depicts characters 'on the razzle'. For that, I made use of popular themes. These themes are strongly 'evocative' . . . Yes, very 'evocative'. Even 'peculiar' . . . the 'timorous' – and other 'moralists' – will reproach me for using these themes. I don't bother with the opinions of such people . . . Reactionary 'muttonheads' will hurl their thunderbolts. Bah! I only permit one judge: the public. They will recognize these themes and will not be the least bit offended in hearing them.[23]

As it turned out, the public judged *Relâche* more harshly than anything Satie had previously done, but for Picabia and avant-garde artists it was 'perfect' and 'a masterpiece', inspiring a rallying cry: 'Long live Satie!'[24]

Envoi

Time passes, and will not pass again.
Satie

In fact, Satie had only months to live. Sick with cirrhosis of the liver, his health declined rapidly during the winter of 1925, and by February he was no longer able to make the daily trip from Arcueil to Paris. Friends arranged a room for him at the luxurious Grand Hôtel on the Place de l'Opéra, thinking that he would like the view, but as Madeleine Milhaud recalled, he 'hated' it and stayed only two days. He spent the next days at the small Hôtel Istria in Montparnasse, a 'very noisy, little place, extremely gay, the type of place where the women who sit for painters have rooms', which Picabia and others working on *Relâche* had made their unofficial headquarters only months earlier.[1] By April he developed pleurisy and had to be hospitalized; Etienne de Beaumont arranged a private room at the Hôpital Saint-Joseph, and it was there that Satie lived out his last days. Among his regular visitors was the young composer Henri Sauget, who left a moving description of Satie during these final months:

I saw him get paler, thinner and weaker, but the bright, piercing look in his eye never faltered. He kept his lively, whimsical sense of humour and his sly, tender smile. When the secretary of his publisher Lerolle brought him a bunch of flowers, he exclaimed 'Already!' . . . no doubt regarding them as an ill omen . . . He passed away peacefully at 8 p.m. on 1 July, after receiving the last rites of the church . . . His last words were 'Ah! The cows . . .'

The funeral took place in Arcueil on 6 July. Francis Poulenc, with whom Satie had broken ties during the Monte Carlo season in 1924, did not attend but instead heard the details in a letter from his friend Raymonde Linoissier. Satie, she wrote, was buried:

> this morning in Arcueil, in a simple, rustic ceremony, where the coffin was lowered straight into the earth – a deal coffin stained red to imitate mahogany . . . No doubt many people were unable to attend, and only the smart, leisured, homosexual set was well represented . . . I feared, and rightly so, that people might not turn up because of the holidays and the remoteness of Arcueil. I also feared that the funeral might be a rather poor affair and I wanted *le bon maître* to be treated as a *maître* and not as a penniless musician . . . there was a touching artificial violet tribute costing about 25 francs with a ribbon bearing the message: 'To Monsieur Satie – The Tenants.' He must have been greatly loved there. The patissière wanted to know all the details of his death.[2]

An article in the next day's issue of *Comoedia* took note of those in attendance, listing Cocteau, Darius and Madeleine Milhaud, Auric, Germaine Tailleferre, Sauget, Paulette Darty, Valentine (née Gross) and Jean Hugo, René Clair and Lucien Vogel among the mourners.[3] Conrad Satie was there as well, and recorded his impressions of the day, ending with a whimsical vision: 'We move away from the burial vault. I hear Satie's bantering voice saying to God: "Just give me time to put on a petticoat, and then I'm yours." He was so alive.'[4]

In the days after the funeral, Conrad, Darius Milhaud and a few other friends gathered again in Arcueil to clear out Satie's apartment. It was apparently the first time in decades that anyone but Satie had entered the room, which by all accounts was in a nightmarish condition. As Milhaud recalled:

A narrow corridor, with a washbasin in it, led to the bedroom into which Satie had never allowed anyone, not even his concierge, to penetrate. It was with a feeling akin to awe that we approached it now. What a shock we had when opening the door! It seemed impossible that Satie lived in such poverty. The man, whose faultlessly clean and correct dress made him look rather like a model civil servant, had literally *nothing* worth a shilling to his name: a wretched bed, a table covered with the most unlikely objects, one chair and a half-empty wardrobe in which there were a dozen old-fashioned corduroy suits, brand-new and almost identical. In each corner of the room there were piles of old newspapers, old hats and walking sticks. On the ancient, broken-down piano with its pedals tied up with string, there was a parcel whose postmark proved it had been delivered several years before: he had merely torn a corner of the paper to see what it contained – a little picture, some New Year's present, no doubt. On the piano we found gifts bearing witness to precious friendship, the *édition de luxe* of Debussy's *Poèmes de Baudelaire*, and *Estampes* and *Images*, with affectionate dedications . . . With his characteristic meticulous care, he had arranged in an old cigar box more than four thousand little pieces of paper on which he had made curious drawings and written extravagant inscriptions. They spoke of enchanted shores, pools and marshes in the time of Charlemagne . . . He had also very carefully traced tiny plans of an imaginary Arcueil, in which the Place du Diable stood very near the Place Notre Dame.[5]

Obituary notices appeared in the Paris press and in major papers worldwide, in many cases harshly assessing the composer and his work. Henri Prunières, editor of *La Revue musicale*, voiced a common view when he claimed that the celebrity Satie enjoyed after World War I had a negative influence on his art; 'His success', the critic opined, 'killed him.'[6] British critic Eric Blom was even more hostile, characterizing Satie as an 'original but ineffectual musician', and a 'preposterous eccentric'.[7] A loyal opposition, including Cocteau, members of Les Six and prominent figures such as Boris de Schloezer and Alfred Cortot, argued 'the Satie case', establishing the foundations for a meaningful assessment of his legacy and setting the stage for a resurgence of interest in Satie that would take hold in the United States in the 1950s. John Cage, in the vanguard of this revival, never wavered in his admiration for the composer he considered to be 'indispensable', not least for his insistent disregard of conventional boundaries. 'To be interested in Satie,' Cage wrote in 1958, 'one must be disinterested to begin with, accept that a sound is a sound and a man is a man, give up illusions about ideas of order, expressions of sentiment, and all the rest of our inherited claptrap.'[8]

Looking back over Satie's career, it becomes clear that the 'inherited' tradition was indeed not for him. He staked out fresh territory from the beginning, forsaking the genres held in highest esteem by musical intellectuals – composing no symphonies, concertos, operas, string quartets or massive keyboard works – and focusing instead on small-scale pieces that challenged the very idea of such conventions. In his music high art meets vernacular idioms, words and music come together in new ways, visual and sonic expressions collide. Engaged equally with the idea of the ancient world and the energy of everyday Paris, he meshed old and new with sophistication, wit and elegance. Utterly original, he was exactly of his time and place, whether as part of the fun-loving *fin de siècle* cabaret scene in Montmartre or the heady postwar avant-garde. At the centre and through it all, there was an aesthetic vision, a deeply personal view of his art, which Satie carefully noted on the cover of one of his sketchbooks while working on *Socrate* in 1917. 'Craftsmanship', he wrote, 'is often superior to subject matter':

> Do not forget that the melody is the Idea, the outline; as much as it is the form and the subject matter of a work. The harmony is an illumination, an exhibition of the object, its reflection.
> Great Masters are brilliant through their ideas, their craft is a simple means to an end, nothing more. It is their ideas which will endure.
> What they achieve is always good and seems natural to us . . .
> Who established the Truths governing Art? Who?
> The Masters. They had no right to do so and it is dishonest to concede this power to them . . .

And, in almost a postscript, he left the statement that not only best encapsulates his aesthetic, but also offers a challenge to all who follow:

> Become Artists unconsciously.
> The Idea can do without Art.
> Let us mistrust Art: it is often nothing but virtuosity.[9]

In the end, Satie was thin and wasted by his illness, seemingly beyond caring about dress or image. Yet in his final days Madeleine Milhaud went to Arcueil to collect fresh laundry from his concierge, gathering what seemed to be an enormous number of handkerchiefs. Returning to the hospital she was surprised to meet an irate Satie, Velvet Gentleman and dandy to the end, who 'blew up again because there were only ninety-eight handkerchiefs when it seemed he had given ninety-nine or a hundred to the laundry'.[10]

References

Introduction

1 Pierre-Daniel Templier, *Erik Satie* (Paris, 1932).
2 *Ibid.*, p. 100.
3 Rollo Myers, *Erik Satie* (London, 1948).
4 Virgil Thomson, *The Musical Scene* (New York, 1947), p. 118.
5 John Cage, 'Satie Controversy', in *John Cage*, ed. Richard Kostelanetz (New York, 1970), p. 90.
6 Roger Shattuck, *The Banquet Years: The Origins of the Avant-Garde in France, 1885 to World War I* (New York, 1968).
7 'Preface to the Vintage Edition', in *ibid*.
8 Author's translation; Satie, 'Mémoires d'un Amnésique (fragments)', *Revue musicale s.i.m.* (15 April 1912), p. 69; reprinted in Erik Satie, *Ecrits*, ed. Ornella Volta (Paris, 1990), p. 19; alternative trans. in Erik Satie, *A Mammal's Notebook*, ed. Ornella Volta, trans. Antony Melville (London, 1996), pp. 101–7.
9 *Ibid.*, p. 101.
10 Satie, *Ecrits*, p. 142.
11 Satie, 'Recoins de ma vie', *Les feuilles libres* (January–February 1924), pp. 329–31; reprinted in Satie, *Ecrits*, p. 25; alternative trans. in Satie, *A Mammal's Notebook*, p. 106.

1 Honfleur

1 Satie, 'Recoins de ma vie', *Les feuilles libres* (January–February 1924), pp. 329–31; reprinted in Erik Satie, *Ecrits*, ed. Ornella Volta (Paris,

1990), p. 25; alternative trans. in Satie, *A Mammal's Notebook*, ed. Ornella Volta, trans. Antony Melville (London, 1996), p. 106.

2 Ornella Volta, *Erik Satie honfleurais* (Honfleur, 1998), p. 12.

3 *Ibid.*, pp. 11–13.

4 Pierre-Daniel Templier, *Erik Satie* (Paris, 1932), p. 7.

5 Ornella Volta, *Satie Seen through his Letters* (London, 1989), p. 16.

6 Templier, *Erik Satie*, p. 7.

7 Volta, *Erik Satie honfleurais*, p. 15.

8 *Ibid.*

9 Satie, 'Recoins de ma vie', reprinted in Satie, *Ecrits*, p. 26; alternative trans. in Satie, *A Mammal's Notebook*, p. 106.

10 Robert Orledge, 'The Musical Activities of Alfred Satie and Eugénie Satie-Barnetche, and their Effects on the Career of Erik Satie', *Journal of the Royal Musical Association*, CXVII/2 (1997), pp. 170–97.

11 Quoted in Templier, *Erik Satie*, pp. 7–8.

12 Robert Orledge, *Satie Remembered* (London, 1995), pp. 10–13.

13 Orledge, 'The Musical Activities of Alfred Satie and Eugénie Satie-Barnetche', pp. 274–5.

14 Steven Moore Whiting, *Satie the Bohemian* (Oxford, 1999), p. 63.

2 Student, Soldier, Gymnopédiste

1 J. P. Contamine de Latour, 'Erik Satie intime: souvenirs de jeunesse', *Comoedia* (August 1925), p. 2; trans. in Robert Orledge, *Satie Remembered* (London, 1995), pp. 15–17.

2 Pierre-Daniel Templier, *Erik Satie* (Paris, 1932), p. 13; trans. in Orledge, *Satie Remembered*, p. 9.

3 *Ibid.*

4 Conrad Satie, 'Erik Satie', *Le Coeur* (June 1895), pp. 2–3; trans. in Orledge, *Satie Remembered*, pp. 48–50.

5 *Ibid.*

6 Orledge, *Satie Remembered*, p. 13.

7 Templier, *Erik Satie*, p. 13; trans. in Orledge, *Satie Remembered*, p. 9.

8 Alexis Roland-Manuel, *Erik Satie: Causerie faite à la Société Lyre et Palette, le 18 Avril 1916* (Paris, 1916), p. 3.

9 Satie, quoted in Paul Collaer, *La musique moderne* (Brussels, 1955); trans.

Sally Abeles as *A History of Modern Music* (Cleveland, 1961), p. 136.

10 Robert Orledge, 'Satie's *Sarabandes* and their Importance to his Composing Career', *Music and Letters*, LXXVII/4 (November 1996), pp. 555–65.

11 Orledge, *Satie the Composer*, p. 36.

12 Templier, *Erik Satie*, p. 14; trans. in Orledge, *Satie Remembered*, p. 9.

13 Templier, *Erik Satie*, p. 15.

14 Description published in *Le Chat Noir*, 8 April 1882; quoted in Philip Denis Cate and Mary Shaw, eds, *The Spirit of Montmartre: Cabarets, Humor, and the Avant-Garde, 1875–1905* (New Brunswick, NJ, 1996), p. 26.

15 Philip Denis Cate, 'The Spirit of Montmartre', in Cate and Shaw, eds, *The Spirit of Montmartre*, pp. 60–62.

16 Contamine de Latour, 'Erik Satie: Souvenires de jeunesse'; trans. in Orledge, *Satie Remembered*, p. 24.

17 *Ibid.*, p. 25.

18 *Ibid.*

19 Francis Jourdain, *Né en 76* (Paris, 1951), pp. 244–8; trans. in Orledge, *Satie Remembered*, p. 39.

20 Latour, 'Erik Satie: Souvenirs de jeunesse'; trans. in Orledge, *Satie Remembered*, p. 25.

21 *Ibid.*, p. 25.

22 Roger Shattuck, *The Banquet Years: The Origins of the Avant-Garde in France, 1885 to World War I* (New York, 1968), p. 141.

23 Quoted in Steven Moore Whiting, *Satie the Bohemian* (Oxford, 1999), pp. 92–3.

24 Reproduced in Ornella Volta, *Satie et la danse* (Paris, 1992), p. 143.

25 Gustave Doret, *Temps et contretemps: Souvenirs d'un musicien* (Fribourg, 1942), p. 98; trans. in Orledge, *Satie Remembered*, p. 47.

26 Louis Laloy, *La musique retrouvée* (Paris, 1928), pp. 258–9; trans. in Orledge, *Satie Remembered*, pp. 98–9; Marc Bredel, *Erik Satie* (Paris, 1982), pp. 84, 90.

27 Jean Cocteau, 'Fragments d'une conférence sur Eric [*sic*] Satie (1920)'; trans. Leigh Henry in *Fanfare*, 1–2 (15 October 1921), p. 23.

28 Satie, 'Claude Debussy', in Satie, *Ecrits*, pp. 65–70; trans. in Wilkins, *The Writings of Erik Satie*, pp. 106–10.

29 *Ibid.*

30 Victor-Emile Michelet, *Les compagnons de la hiérophanie: souvenires du*

mouvement hermétiste à la fin du 19e siècle (Paris, 1937), p. 73; trans. in
Orledge, *Satie Remembered*, pp. 44–5.

31 Quoted in Ornella Volta, *Erik Satie: D'Esoterik Satie à Satierik* (Paris,
1979), p. 139.

32 Whiting, *Satie the Bohemian*, p. 101.

33 *Ibid.*, p. 103.

3 Parcier

1 Contamine de Latour, 'Erik Satie: souvenirs de jeunesse'; trans. in
Robert Orledge, *Satie Remembered* (London, 1995), p. 26.

2 Quoted in *Erik Satie à Montmartre*, exh. cat., Musée de Montmartre,
Paris (1982), pp. 8–9.

3 Stéphane Mallarmé, 'Homage (à Puvis de Chavannes)', *Collected Poems*,
ed. Henry Weinfield (Berkeley, CA, 1994), p. 75.

4 Quoted in Steven Moore Whiting, *Satie the Bohemian* (Oxford, 1999),
p. 120.

5 Fr Aug. Gevaert, *Histoire et théorie de la musique de l'antiquité*, I (Ghent,
1875).

6 Whiting, *Satie the Bohemian*, p. 117.

7 Maria H. Hand, 'Carloz Schwabe's Poster for the Salon de la
Rose+Croix: A Herald of the Ideal in Art,' *Art Journal*, XLIV/1 (Spring
1984), pp. 40–45.

8 Joséphin Péladan, *Le Salon* (Dixième année), pp. 55–6; quoted in Hand,
'Carloz Schwabe's Poster', p. 40.

9 Quoted in Hand, 'Carloz Schwabe's Poster', p. 41.

10 Quoted in Whiting, *Satie the Bohemian*, p. 140.

11 Reproduced in Philip Denis Cate and Mary Shaw, eds, *The Spirit of
Montmartre: Cabarets, Humor, and the Avant-Garde, 1875–1905* (New
Brunswick, NJ, 1996), p. 68.

12 Rusiñol, quoting Satie, in *Erik Satie à Montmartre*, p. 9.

13 Courtney S. Adams, 'Erik Satie and Golden Section Analysis', *Music and
Letters*, LXXVII (1996), pp. 242–52.

14 Quoted in Whiting, *Satie the Bohemian*, p. 128.

15 Quoted in Ornella Volta, *Satie Seen through his Letters* (London, 1989),
p. 60.

16 Nigel Wilkins, *The Writings of Erik Satie* (London, 1980), p. 150.

17 Satie, *Ecrits*, pp. 235–6; trans. in Orledge, *Satie Remembered*, pp. 48–50.

18 Satie, 'Epître d'Erik Satie première aux artistes catholiques et à tous les Chrétiens', *Le Coeur* (September–October 1893), pp. 11–12; reprinted in Satie, *Ecrits*, p. 15; alternative trans. in Satie, *A Mammal's Notebook*, ed. Ornella Volta, trans. Antony Melville (London, 1996), p. 97.

19 Wilkins, *Writings of Erik Satie*, pp. 44–5.

20 Contamine de Latour, 'Erik Satie intime'; trans. in Orledge, *Satie Remembered*, p. 31.

21 Satie, Letter to Suzanne Valadon, 11 March 1893, in *Correspondance presque complète*, ed. Ornella Volta (Paris, 2002), p. 42.

22 Quoted in Volta, *Satie Seen through his Letters*, p. 47.

4 Velvet Gentleman

1 Satie, *Correspondance presque complète*, ed. Ornella Volta (Paris, 2002), p. 53.

2 Satie, Letter to Conrad Satie, [22 July 1896?], *Correspondance*, pp. 72–3.

3 Alan Gillmor, *Erik Satie* (Boston, MA, 1988), p. 46.

4 Quoted in *ibid.*, p. 107.

5 Robert Orledge, *Satie the Composer* (Cambridge, 1990), pp. 190–91.

6 Roger Shattuck, *The Banquet Years: The Origins of the Avant-Garde in France, 1885 to World War I* (New York, 1968), p. 140.

7 Quoted in Ornella Volta, *Satie Seen through his Letters* (London, 1989), p. 70.

8 Roger Shattuck in conversation with John Cage, *Contact*, 25 (1982), p. 25.

9 Pierre-Daniel Templier, *Erik Satie* (Paris, 1932), p. 52.

10 George Auriol, 'Erik Satie, the Velvet Gentleman', *Revue musicale*, 5 (March 1924), pp. 210-11; trans. in Robert Orledge, *Satie Remembered* (London, 1995), pp. 71–2.

11 Pierre de Massot, 'Quelques propos et souvenirs sur Erik Satie', *Revue musicale*, 214 (June 1952), pp. 127–8; trans. in Orledge, *Satie Remembered*, pp. 74–5.

12 Steven Moore Whiting, *Satie the Bohemian* (Oxford, 1999), pp. 184ff.

13 Ornella Volta, *Erik Satie et la tradition populaire* (Paris, 1988), p. 14.

14 Philip Denis Cate and Mary Shaw, eds, *The Spirit of Montmartre:*

Cabarets, Humor, and the Avant-Garde, 1875–1905 (New Brunswick, NJ, 1996), pp. 186–7.

15 Ornella Volta, 'L'Os à moelle: Dossier Erik Satie', *Revue Internationale de Musique française*, VIII/23 (June 1987), pp. 6–31.

16 Darius Milhaud, 'The Death of Erik Satie', trans. Donald Evans in *Notes without Music* (London, 1967), p. 151.

17 Satie, Letter to Conrad Satie, 7 June 1900, *Correspondance*, p. 97.

18 Satie, *Les Musiciens de Montmartre*, trans. and reprinted in Nigel Wilkins, *The Writings of Erik Satie* (London, 1980), p. 6.

19 Ornella Volta, *L'Ymagier d'Erik Satie* (Paris, 1979; reprinted 1990), p. 40.

20 Whiting, *Satie the Bohemian*, p. 257.

21 Paulette Darrty, 'Souvenirs sur Eric Satie'; trans. in Orledge, *Satie Remembered*, p. 96.

22 Whiting, *Satie the Bohemian*, p. 303.

23 See Templier, *Erik Satie*, pp. 25–6.

24 Vladimir Golschmann, 'Golschmann Remembers Erik Satie', *Musical America*, 22 (August 1972), pp. 11–12; trans. in Orledge, *Satie Remembered*, p. 100.

25 Quoted in *ibid.*, p. 11.

26 Satie, Letter to Conrad Satie, 17 January 1911, *Correspondance*, p. 145.

27 Volta, *Satie Seen through his Letters*, pp. 27–8.

5 Scholiste

1 Nigel Wilkins, *The Writings of Erik Satie* (London, 1980), pp. 106–10.

2 Pierre-Daniel Templier, *Erik Satie* (Paris, 1932), p. 27.

3 Quoted in Robert Orledge, *Satie the Composer* (Cambridge, 1990), p. 81; and quoted in Templier, *Erik Satie*, p. 27.

4 Jean Cocteau, 'Fragments d'une conférence sur Eric [*sic*] Satie (1920)', *Revue musicale*, 5 (March 1924), p. 222.

5 Satie, Letter to Conrad Satie, 17 January 1911, *Correspondance presque complète*, ed. Ornella Volta (Paris, 2002), p. 145.

6 Satie, *Ecrits*, ed. Ornella Volta (Paris, 1990), pp. 25–6.

7 Satie, Letter to Conrad Satie, 6 September 1911, *Correspondance*, p. 155.

8 Satie, Letter to Alexis Roland-Manuel, 4 August 1911, *Correspondance*, p. 154.

9 Alan Gillmor, *Erik Satie* (Boston, MA, 1988), p. 137.

10 Ornella Volta, *Satie Seen through his Letters* (London, 1989), p. 85.

6 Bourgeois Radical

1 Quoted in Pierre-Daniel Templier, *Erik Satie* (Paris, 1932), p. 33.

2 Satie, Letter to Conrad Satie, 27 March 1911, *Correspondance presque complète*, ed. Ornella Volta (Paris, 2002), p. 149.

3 Jules Ecorcheville, 'Erik Satie', *Revue musicale s.i.m.*, 7 (15 March 1911), pp. 29–40; Michel Calvocoressi, 'M. Erik Satie', *Musica*, 10 (April 1911), pp. 65–6; Michel Calvocoressi, 'The Origin of To-day's Musical Idiom', *Musical Times*, LII (1 December 1911), pp. 776–7.

4 Satie, Letter to Roland-Manuel, 3 July 1912, *Correspondance*, p. 170.

5 Satie, *Ecrits*, ed. Ornella Volta (Paris, 1990), p. 158.

6 For an extensive sampling of these designs, see *ibid.*, pp. 184–228.

7 Jean Wiéner, 'Un grand musicien', *Arts*, I/25 (20 July 1945), p. 4.

8 Quoted in Victor Du Bled, *La Société française du xvie siècle au xxe siècle. ix Série: xviiie et xixe siècles: Le Premier salon de France: L'Académie française: L'Argot* (Paris, 1913), p. 258.

9 Guillaume Apollinaire, *Calligrammes: Poems of Peace and War (1913–1916)*, ed. Anne Greet and S. I. Lockerbie, trans. Anne Greet (Berkeley, CA, 1980), pp. 4–5.

10 Apollinaire, 'Lundi, rue Christine', *Les Soirées de Paris* (December 1913); reprinted in *ibid.*, p. 52.

11 Templier, *Erik Satie*, p. 82.

12 'Le Golf', *Fémina*, 15 May 1913, p. 267; 'La coupe Fémina', *Fémina*, May 1921, p. 36.

13 'Vernissage cubiste', *Cri de Paris*, quoted in Billy Klüver and Julie Martin, *Kiki's Paris: Artists and Lovers, 1900–1930* (New York, 1989), p. 222 n. 4.

14 Alexis Roland-Manuel, *Erik Satie* (n. p.).

15 Quoted in Arthur Gold and Robert Fitzdale, *Misia: The Life of Misia Sert* (New York, 1980), p. 174.

16 'A New Salon for Unique Fashions', *Vogue* [New York], 1 October 1912, p. 47.

7 Ballets Russes

1 Quoted in Frederick Brown, *An Impersonation of Angels: A Biography of Jean Cocteau* (New York, 1968), p. 87.

2 Richard Axsom, *Parade: Cubism as Theater* (New York, 1979), fig. 96.

3 Régis Gignoux, 'Courrier des théâtres – avant première', *Le Figaro*, 18 May 1917, p. 4.

4 Jean d'Udine, 'Couleurs, mouvements, et sons: Les Ballets Russes en 1917', *Le Courrier musical*, June 1917, p. 239.

5 Guillaume Apollinaire, '"Parade" et l'esprit nouveau', *L'Excelsior*, 11 May 1917, p. 5.

6 Ernest Newman, *The Observer*, 23 November 1919; quoted in Deborah Menaker Rothschild, *Picasso's Parade: From Street to Stage* (New York, 1991), p. 95.

7 The Berlin/Satie meeting in 1922 is reported in Gaige Crosby, *Footlights and Highlights* (New York, 1948), p. 186.

8 See Satie, copyist's manuscript for *Parade*, p. 1 (Frederick R. Koch Foundation, Beinecke Rare Book and Manuscript Library, Yale University, New Haven)

9 Jean Cocteau, '"Parade": Ballet réaliste, In Which Four Modern Artists Had a Hand', *Vanity Fair*, September 1917, p. 37.

10 *Ibid.*

11 Jean Cocteau, *Le Coq et l'arlequin* (Paris, 1918, reprinted 1979).

12 Carl Van Vechten, 'Erik Satie: Master of the Rigolo', *Vanity Fair*, March 1918, p. 61.

13 Erik Satie, 'A Hymn in Praise of Critics, Those Whistling Bell-Buoys Who Indicate the Reefs on the Shores of the Human Spirit', *Vanity Fair*, September 1921, p. 49.

14 Erik Satie, 'A Lecture on "The Six": A Somewhat Critical Account of a Now Famous Group of French Musicians', *Vanity Fair*, October 1921, p. 61.

15 Erik Satie, 'A Learned Lecture on Music and Animals', *Vanity Fair*, May 1922, p. 64; Satie, 'La Musique et les enfants', *Vanity Fair*, October 1922, p. 53.

16 Erik Satie, 'Igor Stravinsky: A Tribute to the Great Russian Composer by an Eminent French Confrère', *Vanity Fair*, February 1923, p. 39; Erik Satie, 'Claude Debussy', *Ecrits*, ed. Ornella Volta (Paris, 1990), p. 65.

8 En 'Smoking'

1 Quoted in Sylvia Kahan, *Music's Modern Muse: A Life of Winnaretta Singer, Princesse de Polignac* (Rochester, NY, 2003), pp. 203–4.

2 Satie, Letter to Alexis Rouart, 4 October 1917, *Correspondance presque complète*, ed. Ornella Volta (Paris, 2002), p. 309.

3 Satie, Letter to Valentine Gross, 6 January 1917, *Correspondance*, p. 274.

4 Satie, Letter to Valentine Gross, 18 January 1917, *Correspondance*, pp. 277–8.

5 Satie, Letter to Jean Cocteau, 1 January 1917, *Correspondance*, p. 271.

6 Ornella Volta, *Satie Seen through his Letters* (London, 1989), p. 132.

7 Satie, Postcard to Jean Poueigh, 30 May 1917, *Correspondance*, p. 289.

8 Quoted in Volta, *Satie Seen through his Letters*, p. 140.

9 Satie, Letter to Winnaretta Singer, 10 October 1918, *Correspondance*, pp. 340–41.

10 Satie, Letter to Henry Prunières, 3 April 1918, *Correspondance*, p. 324.

11 Satie, Letter to Valentine Gross, 24 June 1918, *Correspondance*, p. 329.

12 Maurice Sachs, *Au Temps du Boeuf sur le Toit* (Paris, 1948), pp. 29–30.

13 Quoted in Robert Orledge, *Satie the Composer* (Cambridge, 1990), p. 133.

14 Quoted in Alan Gillmor, *Erik Satie* (Boston, MA, 1988), p. 218.

15 *Ibid.*, p. 217.

16 Satie, *Ecrits*, ed. Ornella Volta (Paris, 1990), p. 251.

17 Satie, Letter to Paul Collaer, 16 May 1920, *Correspondance*, pp. 406–7.

18 Pierre Leroi, 'Festival Erik Satie', *Le Courrier musical* (August/September 1920), p. 233.

19 Satie, Letter to Etienne de Beaumont, 11 June 1920, *Correspondance*, p. 411.

20 Morand, quoted in Volta, *Satie Seen through his Letters*, p. 153; Valentine Hugo, 'Le Socrate que j'ai connu', *Revue musicale*, 214 (June 1952), pp. 139–44.

21 Satie, Letter to Madame Claude Debussy, 8 March 1917, *Correspondance*, p. 282.

22 Satie, Letter to Henry Prunières, 3 April 1918, *Correspondance*, p. 324.

23 Satie, Letter to Alexis Roland-Manuel, 14 March 1918, *Correspondance*, pp. 321–2.

24 Quoted in Robert Orledge, *Satie Remembered* (London, 1995), pp. 77–8.

25 Satie, Letter to Valentine Gross, 23 August 1918, *Correspondance*, p. 334.

26 Quoted in Rollo Myers, *Erik Satie* (New York, 1968), p. 60.

27 Darius Milhaud, 'Lettre de Darius Milhaud', *Revue musicale*, 214 (June 1952), p. 153.

28 *Ibid.*, pp. 154–5.

29 J.R.F., 'Conseils d'été', *Vogue* [Paris], 15 June 1920, p. 15.

30 Raymond Radiguet, *Le Bal du Comte d'Orgel* (Paris, 1924); trans. Annapaola Cancogni (New York, 1989).

31 Reginald Bridgeman, quoted in Francis Steegmuller, *Cocteau: A Biography* (Boston, MA, 1970), p. 227.

32 Satie, Letter to Countess Edith de Beaumont, 26 December 1922, *Correspondance*, p. 511.

9 Dadaist

1 Quoted in Ornella Volta, *L'Ymagier d'Erik Satie* (Paris, 1979; reprinted 1990), p. 79.

2 Quoted in Pierre de Massot, 'Vingt-cinq minutes avec: Erik Satie', *Paris-Journal* (30 May 1924), p. 2.

3 Ornella Volta, *Satie Seen through his Letters* (London, 1989), p. 172.

4 Michel Sanouillet, *Dada à Paris* (Paris, 1952), pp. 319–47.

5 Volta, *Satie Seen through his Letters*, p. 186.

6 J.R.F., 'The Maecanas of Paris Entertains', *Vogue* [New York], 1 June 1924, p. 46.

7 'Palmyre reçoit sa Famille: Ses Escapades dans le monde des artistes', *Vogue* [Paris], 1 June 1923, pp. 40–41.

8 Satie, Letter to Darius Milhaud, 15 September 1923, *Correspondance presque complète*, ed. Ornella Volta (Paris, 2002), p. 561.

9 Ornella Volta, *Satie/Cocteau: Les Malentendus d'une entente* (Paris, 1998), p. 58.

10 Volta, *Satie Seen through his Letters*, p. 179.

11 Quoted in *ibid.*, p. 180.

12 *Ibid.*, p. 181.

13 Sanouillet, *Dada à Paris*, pp. 382–5.

14 Roger Vitrac, quoted in Volta, *Satie Seen through his Letters*, p. 184.

15 Documented in correspondence between Pierre de Massot and Picabia; see *ibid.*, pp. 190–91.

16 Satie, Letter to Francis Picabia, 8 February 1924, *Correspondance*, p. 587.

17 Martin Marks, 'The Well-Furnished Film: Satie's Score for Entr'acte', *Canadian University Music Review*, 4 (1983), pp. 245–77.

18 Satie, Letter to Pierre Massot, 27 July [1924], *Correspondance*, pp. 625–6.

19 Volta, *Satie Seen through his Letters*, p. 196.

20 Roland-Manuel, 'Adieu à Satie', *Revue Pleyel*, 15 (December 1924), pp. 21–2.

21 Robert Orledge, *Satie the Composer* (Cambridge, 1990), pp. 177–84.

22 Marks, 'The Well-Furnished Film', p. 250.

23 Satie, trans. and quoted in Orledge, *Satie the Composer*, p. 357, n. 17.

24 Picabia, quoted in Robert Orledge, *Satie Remembered* (London, 1995), p. 194.

Envoi

1 Madeleine Milhaud, quoted in Robert Orledge, *Satie Remembered* (London, 1995), pp. 212–13.

2 Raymonde Linoissier, Letter to Francis Poulenc; in *ibid.*, *Satie Remembered*, pp. 218–19.

3 *Ibid.*, pp. 216–17.

4 *Ibid.*, p. 220.

5 *Ibid*., pp. 214–15.

6 Henri Prunières, 'The Failure of Success', *Musical Digest*, 8 (28 July 1925), p. 5.

7 Eric Blom, 'Erik Satie (1866–1925)', *Musical News and Herald*, 69 (18 July 1925), p. 53.

8 John Cage, 'On Erik Satie', *Art News Annual*, XXVII (1958), p. 81; reprinted in John Cage, *Silence* (Middletown, CT, 1961), p. 82.

9 Satie, *Ecrits*, ed. Ornella Volta (Paris, 1990), pp. 48–9; trans. in Robert Orledge, *Satie the Composer* (Cambridge, 1990), pp. 68–9.

10 Quoted in Orledge, *Satie Remembered*, p. 213.

Bibliography

Autograph sources

Most of Satie's autograph manuscripts are housed in the collections of the
Bibliothèque Nationale de France, Paris, and at the Houghton Library,
Harvard University. A chronological list of compositions included in Robert
Orledge's *Satie the Composer* offers a useful summary of Satie's output,
including information concerning manuscript location, publication history
and premiere performances.

Writings

Satie's published writings appeared during his lifetime in a variety of magazines and journals in France and the United States. They have since been collected and issued with his private commentaries, notes and small jottings in
a number of French and English sources.

Satie, Erik, *Ecrits*, ed. Ornella Volta (Paris, 1990)
——, *Les Bulles du Parcier*, ed. Ornella Volta (Frontfroide, 1991)
——, *A Mammal's Notebook*, ed. Ornella Volta, trans. Antony Melville
    (London, 1996)
Wilkins, Nigel, *The Writings of Erik Satie* (London, 1980)

Letters

Borgeaud, Henri, 'Trois lettres d'Erik Satie à Claude Debussy (1903)', *Revue de Musicologie*, XLVIII (1962), pp. 71–4

Lockspeiser, Edward, *The Literary Clef: An Anthology of Letters and Writings by French Composers* (London, 1958)

Satie, Erik, *Correspondance presque complète*, ed. Ornella Volta (Paris, 2002)

Volta, Ornella, *Satie Seen through his Letters* (London, 1989)

Wilkins, Nigel, 'Erik Satie's Letters', *Canadian University Music Review*, II (1981), pp. 207–27

——, 'Erik Satie's Letters to Milhaud and Others', *Musical Quarterly*, LXVI (1980), pp. 404–28

Iconography

Volta, Ornella, *L'Ymagier d'Erik Satie* (Paris, 1990)

——, *Erik Satie* (Paris, 1997)

Satie's life and music

Adams, Courtney, 'Erik Satie and Golden Section Analysis', *Music and Letters*, LXXVII (1996), pp. 242–52

Apollinaire, Guillaume, '"Parade" et l'esprit nouveau', *L'Excelsior* (11 May 1917), p. 5

——, *Calligrammes: Poems of Peace and War (1913–1916)*, ed. Anne Greet and S. I. Lockerbie, trans. Anne Greet (Berkeley, CA, 1980)

Axsom, Richard, *Parade: Cubism as Theater* (New York, 1979)

Blom, Eric, 'Erik Satie (1866–1925)', *Musical News and Herald*, 69 (18 July 1925), p. 53

Bois, Jules, *Les petites religions de Paris* (Paris, 1894)

Bredel, Marc, *Erik Satie* (Paris, 1982)

Brown, Frederick, *An Impersonation of Angels: A Biography of Jean Cocteau* (New York, 1968)

Cage, John, *Silence* (Middletown, CT, 1969)

Cate, Phillip Dennis, and Mary Shaw, eds, *The Spirit of Montmartre: Cabarets, Humor, and the Avant-Garde, 1875–1905* (New Brunswick, NJ, 1996)

Cocteau, Jean, '"Parade": Ballet réaliste, in which Four Modern Artists Had a Hand', *Vanity Fair* (September 1917), p. 37

——, 'Fragments d'une conférence sur Eric [*sic*] Satie (1920)', *Revue musicale*, V (March 1924), p. 222

——, *Portraits-Souvenirs, 1900–14* (Paris, 1935); trans. Jesse Browner as *Souvenir Portraits: Paris in the Belle Epoque* (London, 1991)

——, *Erik Satie* (Liège, 1957)

——, *Le Coq et l'arlequin* (Paris, 1918, reprinted 1978)

Collaer, Paul, *La musique moderne* (Brussels, 1955); trans. Sally Abeles as *A History of Modern Music* (Cleveland, 1961)

Contamine de Latour, J.P., 'Erik Satie intime: Souvenirs de jeunesse', *Comoedia*, 3, 5 and 6 August 1925

Cooper, Douglas, *Picasso Theater* (New York, 1987)

Crosby, Gaige, *Footlights and Highlights* (New York, 1948)

Davis, Mary E., *Classic Chic: Music, Fashion, and Modernism* (Berkeley, CA, 2006)

——. 'Modernity à la mode: Popular Culture and Avant-gardism in Erik Satie's *Sports et divertissements*', *Musical Quarterly*, 83 (Fall 1999), pp. 430–73

Donnay, Maurice, *Autour du Chat Noir* (Paris, 1926, reprinted 1996)

Ecorcheville, Jules, 'Erik Satie', *Revue musicale S.I.M.*, 7 (15 March 1911), pp. 29–40

Erik Satie à Montmartre, exh. cat., Musée de Montmartre, Paris (1982)

Garafola, Lynn, *Diaghilev's Ballets Russes* (Oxford, 1989)

Gignoux, Régis, 'Courrier des théâtres – avant-première', *Le Figaro* (18 May 1917), p. 5

Gillmor, Alan, *Erik Satie* (Boston, MA, 1988)

Gold, Arthur, and Robert Fitzdale, *Misia: The Life of Misia Sert* (New York, 1980)

Gowers, Patrick, 'Satie's Rose-Croix Music (1891–1895)', *Proceedings of the Royal Music Association*, XCII (1965–6), pp. 1–25

——, 'Erik Satie: His Studies, Notebooks, and Critics,' PhD dissertation, University of Cambridge, 1966

Hand, Maria H, 'Carlos Schwabe's Poster for the Salon Rose + Croix: A

Herald of the Ideal in Art', *Art Journal*, XLIV/1 (Spring 1984), pp. 40–45

Harding, James, *Erik Satie* (New York, 1975)

Hugo, Valentine, 'Le Socrate que j'ai connu', *Revue musicale*, 214 (June 1952), pp. 139–45

Kahan, Sylvia, *Music's Modern Muse: A Life of Winnaretta Singer, Princesse de Polignac* (Rochester, NY, 2003)

Jean-Aubry, Georges, *French Music of Today*, trans. Edwin Evans (London, 1919)

Kostelanetz, Richard, ed., *John Cage* (New York, 1970)

Klüver, Billy, and Julie Martin, *Kiki's Paris: Artists and Lovers, 1900–1930* (New York, 1989)

Lajoinie, Vincent, *Erik Satie* (Lausanne, 1985)

Leroi, Pierre, 'Festival Erik Satie', *Le Courrier musical* (August–September 1920), p. 233

Mallarmé, Stéphane, *Collected Poems*, ed. Henry Weinfield (Berkeley, CA, 1994)

Marks, Martin, 'The Well-Furnished Film: Satie's Score for *Entr'acte*', *Canadian University Music Review*, 4 (1983), pp. 245–77

Massot, Pierre de, 'Vingt-cinq minutes avec: Erik Satie', *Paris-Journal*, 30 May 1924, p. 2

Messing, Scott, *Neoclassicism in Music: From the Genesis of the Concept through the Schoenberg/Stravinsky Polemic* (Ann Arbor, MI, 1988)

Milhaud, Darius, *Ma vie heureuse* (Paris, 1973)

——, *Notes without Music: An Autobiography*, trans. Donald Evans (New York, 1953)

Myers, Rollo, *Erik Satie* (London, 1948, reprinted New York, 1969)

Nichols, Roger, *The Harlequin Years: Music in Paris, 1917–1929* (Berkeley, CA, 2003)

Orledge, Robert, *Satie the Composer* (Cambridge, 1990)

——, 'The Musical Activities of Alfred Satie and Eugénie Satie-Barnetche, and their Effect on the Career of Erik Satie', *Journal of the Royal Musical Association*, CXVII/2 (1992), pp. 270–92

——, 'Satie and the Art of Dedication', *Music and Letters*, LXXIII (1992), pp. 551–64

——, *Satie Remembered* (London, 1995)

——, 'Satie's Sarabandes and their Importance to his Composing Career', *Music and Letters*, LXXVII/4 (November 1996), pp. 555–65

——, 'Erik Satie's Ballet "Mercure" (1924): From Mount Etna to Montmartre', *Journal of the Royal Musical Association*, cxxiii/2 (1998), pp. 229–49

——, 'Satie in America', *American Music*, xviii/1 (Spring 2000), pp. 909–12

Perloff, Nancy, *Art and the Everyday: Popular Entertainment and the Circle of Erik Satie* (New York, 1991)

Poulenc, Francis, *My Friends and Myself*, trans. Cynthia Jolly (London, 1978)

Prunières, Henri, 'The Failure of Success', *Musical Digest*, 8 (25 July 1925), p. 5

Radiguet, Raymond, *Le Bal du Comte d'Orgel* (Paris, 1924); trans. Annapaola Cancogni as *Count D'Orgel's Ball* (New York, 1989)

Rey, Anne, *Erik Satie* (Paris, 1974)

Roland-Manuel, Alexis, *Erik Satie. Causerie faite à la Société Lyre et Palette, le 18 Avril 1916* (Paris, 1916)

——, 'Adieu à Satie', *Revue Pleyel*, 15 (15 December 1924), pp. 21–2

Rothschild, Deborah Menaker, *Picasso's Parade: From Street to Stage* (New York, 1989)

Sachs, Maurice, *Au temps du Boeuf sur le toit* (Paris, 1939, reprinted 2005)

Sanouillet, Michel, *Dada à Paris* (Paris, 1965)

Satie, Conrad, 'Erik Satie', *Le Coeur* (June 1895), pp. 2–3

Séré, Octave [pseud. of Jean Poueigh], *Musiciens français d'aujourd'hui* (Paris, 1921)

Shattuck, Roger, *The Banquet Years: The Origins of the Avant-Garde in France, 1885 to World War I* (New York, 1958, rvd 1968)

Steegmuller, Francis, *Cocteau: A Biography* (Boston, MA, 1970)

Templier, Pierre-Daniel, *Erik Satie* (Paris, 1932); trans. David and Elena French (Cambridge, MA, 1969)

Thomson, Virgil, *The Musical Scene* (New York, 1947)

Van Vechten, Carl, 'Erik Satie: Master of the Rigolo', *Vanity Fair* (March 1918), p. 61

Volta, Ornella, *Erik Satie: d'Esoterik Satie à Satierik* (Paris, 1979)

——, 'Dossier Erik Satie: L'Os à moëlle', *Revue Internationale de Musique Française*, 23 (June 1987), pp. 7–98

——, *Erik Satie et la tradition populaire* (Paris, 1988)

——, *Satie et la danse* (Paris, 1992)

——, *Satie/Cocteau: les Malentendus d'une entente* (Paris, 1993)

——, *Erik Satie: Bibliographie raisonnée* (Arcueil, 1995)

——, et al., *Erik Satie del Chat Noir a Dadá* (Valencia, 1996)

——, *Erik Satie honfleurais* (Honfleur, 1998)

Wehmeyer, Grete, *Erik Satie* (Regensburg, 1974)

Whiting, Steven Moore, 'Erik Satie and Vincent Hyspa: Notes on a
    Collaboration', *Music and Letters*, LXXVII (1996), pp. 64–91

——, *Satie the Bohemian* (Oxford, 1999)

Select Discography

Compilations

The Very Best of Satie, 2 CDS. Klara Kormendi, Gabor Eckhardt; Nancy Symphony Orchestra, dir. Jerome Kaltenbach. Naxos 8.552137-38. Released 2006.

Piano Music

COMPLETE WORKS

Jean-Joel Barbier, *Satie: Intégrale pour piano*, 4 CDS. Accord 20072, 221362, 220742, 200902. Recorded 1963–71.

Aldo Ciccolini, *Satie: Works for Piano*, 5 CDS. EMI Classics CDC 749702 2, 749703 2, 749713 2, 749714 2, 749760 2. Duets with Gabriel Tacchino. Recorded 1980s.

Jean-Yves Thibaudet, *Satie: Complete Solo Piano Music*, 5 CDS. Decca 473 620-5 DCS. Recorded 2003.

SELECTIONS

Aldo Ciccolini, *Satie: Piano Works*, 2 CDS. EMI Classics CZS 7 67282 2. Recorded 1966–76.

Michel Legrand, *Erik Satie by Michel Legrand*. Erato 4509-92857-2. Recorded 1993.

Anne Queffélec, *Erik Satie* and *Erik Satie: Piano Works*. Virgin Classics 7 90754 2 and 7 59296 2. Recorded 1988 and 1990.

Pascal Rogé, *Satie: Trois Gymnopédies and Other Piano Works*. Decca 410 220-2. Recorded 1983.

Marcela Roggeri, *Satie: Piano Works*. Transart Live, TR 134. Recorded 2005.

Jean-Yves Thibaudet, *The Magic of Satie*. Decca 470 290-2. Recorded 2002.

DUETS

Jean-Pierre Armengaud and Dominique Merlet, *Erik Satie: Complete Works for Piano Duet*. Mandala 4882. Recorded 1996.

Champion-Vachon Duo, *Erik Satie: Complete Works for Piano 4 Hands*. Analekta-Fleur de Lys 2-3040. Recorded 1995.

BALLETS AND ORCHESTRAL MUSIC

The Complete Ballets of Erik Satie. The Utah Symphony Orchestra, dir. Maurice Abravenel. Vanguard Classics OVC 4030. Recorded 1968.

Erik Satie and Darius Milhaud. London Festival Players, dir. Bernard Hermann. London/Decca 443 897-2. Recorded 1996.

Les Inspirations Insolites d'Erik Satie. L'Orchestre de Paris, dir. Pierre Dervaux. EMI Classics CZS 762877 2. Recorded 1966–73.

Satie: Parade, Relâche, En Habit de Cheval. Orchestre du Capitole de Toulouse, dir. Michel Plasson. EMI Classics 749471 2. Recorded 1988.

Satie: Parade, Relâche, Mercure. The New London Orchestra, dir. Ronald Corp. Hyperion CD A66365. Recorded 1989.

VOCAL MUSIC

Satie: Mélodies. Mady Mesplé, Nicolai Gedda, Gariel Bacquier, Aldo Ciccolini. EMI CD 7491672. Recorded 1960s through 1980s.

Satie: Intégrale des Mélodies et des Chansons. Bruno Laplante, Marc Durand. Analekta 1002. Recorded 1986.

Erik Satie: Melodies and Songs. Anne-Sophie Schmidt and Jeanne-Pierre Armengaud. Mandala 4867. Recorded 1996.

ORGAN MUSIC

La Musique mediévale d'Erik Satie. Hervé Desarbre (organ) with the Paris Renaissance Ensemble, dir Hélène Breuil. Includes the *Messe des Pauvres*. Mandala 4896. Recorded 1997.

ARRANGEMENTS AND ADAPTATIONS

The Minimalism of Erik Satie. Vienna Art Orchestra. Harmonia Mundi 6024. Recorded 1989.

Satie: Works for 10-String Guitar. Pierre Laniau. Gramophone 4729672. Recorded 1998.

Satie: Gymnopédies–Gnossiennes. Jacques Loussier Trio. Telarc CD-83431. Recorded 1998.

Sketches of Satie. John Hackett (piano) and Steve Hackett (flute). Camino CAM CD20. Recorded 2000.

Blood, Sweat & Tears. Blood, Sweat & Tears. Mobile Fidelity CMOB 2009 SA. Recorded 1968, reissued in SACD 2005.

OF HISTORICAL INTEREST

Francis Poulenc Plays Satie and Poulenc. Sony Masterworks Portrait MPK 47684. Recorded 1951.

Mélodies. Pierre Bernac and Francis Poulenc. Sony Masterworks Portrait MPK 46731. Recorded 1940s and '50s.

Socrate/Cheap Imitation. Hilke Helling, Deborah Richards, Herbert Henke. Wergo 6186. Recorded 1969.

Acknowledgements

This biography was possible thanks to work done over the past several decades by a community of Satie scholars. Leading the ranks is Ornella Volta, President of the Fondation Erik Satie in Paris, whose countless contributions and great enthusiasm for the composer have proved invaluable and endlessly inspiring. I also wish to thank Daniel Albright, Alan Gillmor, Nancy Perloff, Robert Orledge, and Steven Moore Whiting for their meticulous and perceptive studies of Satie, which have informed my work at fundamental levels. At Reaktion Books, I am indebted to Vivian Constantinopoulos, who commissioned this book, to Harry Gilonis, and to David Rose, for the many improvements he made as it came to fruition. Finally, I wish to thank Reinhold Brinkmann, to whom this book is dedicated, for his longstanding guidance and encouragement.

Photo Acknowledgements

The author and publishers wish to express their thanks to the following sources of illustrative material and/or permission to reproduce it (some locations of artworks are also given below):

Photos Archives de la Fondation Erik Satie, Paris: pp. 14, 16, 23; photos Bibliothèque Nationale de France, Paris: pp. 28, 29, 34, 45, 46, 50, 54, 69; Bibliothèque Nationale de France, Paris: p. 53 (photo Snark/Art Resource, New York); photos © CNAC/MNAM/Dist. Réunion des Musées Nationaux/ Art Resource New York/Artist Rights Society/ADAGP): pp. 6, 57, 133; photo Giroudon/Art Resource, New York/Artist Rights Society/ADAGP p. 60; photos Houghton Library, Harvard University: pp. 95, 96, 97, 99, 100, 101, 150; photos Library of Congress, Washington, DC: pp. 24 (Prints and Photographs Division, LC-USZ62-133247), 111; Musée de l'Orsay, Paris: p. 42 (photo Erich Lessing/Art Resource, New York); Musée National d'Art Moderne, Paris: p. 6 (photo by Man Ray, 1922), 57, 123; Museu Nacional de Arte de Catalunya, Barcelona: p. 32 (photo Artist Rights Society/ADAGP); Museum of Modern Art, New York: p. 138 (digital image © The Museum of Modern Art, New York/licensed by SCALA/Art Resource, New York/ Artist Rights Society/ADAGP); photo Northwestern University Library, Northwestern University, Evanston, Illinois: p. 44; photo Réunion des Musées Nationaux/Art Resource, New York: p. 30; photo Réunion des Musées Nationaux/Art Resource, New York/Artist Rights Society/ADAGP: p. 77; photo Scala/Art Resource, New York/Artist Rights Society/ADAGP: p. 123; photo Vanity Fair/Condé Nast Publications: p. 116.